Development, Crises and Alternative Visions:
Third World Women's Perspectives

Development, Crises and Alternative Visions

Third World Women's Perspectives

by GITA SEN and CAREN GROWN

for Development Alternatives with Women for a New Era
(DAWN)

EARTHSCAN PUBLICATIONS LTD

LONDON

This book was written by Gita Sen and Caren Grown for the project Development Alternatives with Women for a New Era (DAWN). Substantive guidance was provided by the project's Founding Committee and by a large number of women researchers and activists.

First published in Great Britain 1988 by
Earthscan Publications Limited
3 Endsleigh Street, London WC1H 0DD

Published in the USA by Monthly Review Press

British Library Cataloguing in Publication Data

Sen, Gita
    Development, crises and alternative
    visions : Third World women's perspectives.
    1. Developing countries. Women. Social
    conditions
    I. Title   II. Grown, Caren
    305.4′2′091724

    ISBN 1-85383-000-3

Printed and bound in Great Britain by
Cox & Wyman Ltd, Reading

Front cover photograph: Mark Edwards—Still Pictures/Earthscan
Back cover photograph: Maggie Murray
Cover design: David King

Dedicated to the poor and oppressed women of the world
whose anonymous struggles are the building blocks
of a new society

Contents

Preamble

This book constitutes the first stage of a program undertaken by DAWN, a network of activists, researchers, and policymakers. Through our analysis and activities, we are committed to developing alternative frameworks and methods to attain the goals of economic and social justice, peace, and development free of all forms of oppression by gender, class, race, and nation. Most participants draw their experiences from action and research within the women's movements of the past ten years; yet we intend this effort to be inclusive of all those who share in our broad visions for society.

This project, Development Alternatives with Women for a New Era (DAWN), has grown from small seeds planted in Bangalore, India, in August 1984. At that time a nucleus of committed women from a number of different countries came together to share their experiences with development strategies, policies, theories, and research. They questioned the impact of development on poor people, especially women, particularly in light of the global economic and political crises, and voiced a sense of urgency regarding the need to advocate alternative development processes that would give principal emphasis to the basic survival needs of the majority of the world's people. The group recognized the commonality and power of the global economic and political processes that set the context for diverse national and regional experiences, and that often constrain the possibilities for alternative strategies and actions. The experiences of many of the DAWN founders with grassroots initiatives at the community level strengthened their resolve to seek to comprehend such actions within a broader perspective: to link, as it were, the micro-level activities to a macro-level perspective. The group also affirmed that it is the experiences lived by poor women throughout the

Third World in their struggles to ensure the basic survival of their families and themselves that provide the clearest lens for an understanding of development processes. And it is *their* aspirations and struggles for a future free of the multiple oppressions of gender, class, race, and nation that can form the basis for the new visions and strategies that the world now needs.

A "platform" document that would, at one and the same time, articulate such a perspective and also serve to carry forward the debate on alternative development strategies was seen by the group as an important beginning. It must be emphasized that much of the in-depth research and analysis that will deepen our understanding of development from the vantage point of poor Third World women still needs to be done. This book represents, therefore, but a stage in a longer search for new approaches to development. We know that the tentativeness of the discussion and suggestions put forth in the final chapter reflects the unfinished character of the collective search for alternatives. What is presented here is not a finished blueprint, but a small step in a much longer process.

This book was written through extensive debate and discussion with researchers, activists, and policymakers in the year prior to the third United Nations conference marking the United Nations Decade for the Advancement of Women. We consciously attempted to adopt an open and flexible process throughout. This has proven to be a pragmatic and fruitful way of drawing upon varied experiences, germinating new possibilities, and effectively advocating common perspectives and aims. The group's emphasis on the importance of the process arises from its recognition that the nature of our vision of a better society is powerfully influenced by the methods adopted to achieve it. If we ourselves can evolve new working styles, new forms of cooperative organization and practices, this will contribute to the search for genuine alternatives. To build a social order that is just, equitable, and life-affirming for all people, our methods must correspondingly be open and respectful of differences, and must try to break down hierarchies, power, and distrust.

The group wished particularly to open the process to the oppressed women of the Third World. The fact that the DAWN project as a whole was initiated in the Third World and continues to be rooted there has strengthened its appeal to many and encouraged their participation. At the same time, the process has also drawn on the energy, spirit, and resources of committed individuals, sympathetic institutions, and parts of the women's movement in the more industrialized countries. It has also attracted the interest of many oppressed and poor women there, who see in DAWN's analysis and aims an affirmation of their own experiences and visions of a better life.

Many individuals and groups have therefore given unstintingly of their time, experiences, knowledge, and creativity. They nurtured this document as a single collective effort. Often, to the surprise of those involved in its evolution, women and men of differing ideologies but similar commitments to the goals of economic and social transformation have been able to find within DAWN common understandings about the broad issues of development and the meanings of feminism. We wish to stress that the collective process which produced both this book and ongoing DAWN activities reflects the true ethos and potential of the women's movement – an ethos that respects diversity, breaks down hierarchies and competition, and fosters sharing and reciprocity.

The process of outreach and engagement has taken different forms. Numerous conferences and seminars were held in all five continents after the Bangalore meeting to allow as many views and experiences as possible to be debated and incorporated into this text. In Bangalore, the founding group also planned a related series of activities for the U.N.-sponsored Non-Governmental Forum, held in Nairobi, Kenya, in July 1985. DAWN's panels and workshops at the Forum – on the effects of growth-oriented development, the economic, political, and cultural crises, and alternative visions and methods for women's movements – provided an arena for continued debate, discussion, and elaboration of these issues. Additional activities on women and the media and dialogues on various aspects of feminism and on socialism were held to widen the participation and interaction among women. Drama, audio-visuals, and songs enlivened the discussions and further drew out the links between such macro-level phenomena as the global debt crisis and women's lives. By the Forum's end, over two thousand women had participated in panels and workshops and endorsed DAWN's vision and goals. Subsequently, key research and training institutes, international agencies, and development organizations have incorporated this book into their curricula and field work, and women's organizations have attempted to rework and adapt it for use at the grassroots level.

To consider the project's future, the DAWN founders met again in Brazil in February 1986 to set up a structure that would support the group's ongoing activities and broaden participation with the same free flow of ideas and action. Creating a structure while retaining the flexibility of the process proved to be no easy task. The group selected a seven-member steering committee, consisting of a general coordinator and convenors of working groups in the areas of research, publications, advocacy, training, international relations, and communications. These working groups are inter-regional; over the next two years they will carry out multiple tasks focusing on two topics: the food, energy, and debt crises in relation to women, and women's visions and movements in the Third World. It was decided that DAWN is not, at present, a membership organization, but is continuing its activities through consultative processes similar to those used thus far. The original members will retain their advisory role as the Founding Committee. The steering committee and convenors of working groups are drawn from Third World countries. While the primary focus of DAWN's activities remains the Third World, we hope that individuals and grassroots groups in the North can use and develop DAWN's perspectives within their own contexts and share their insights to enrich the DAWN process.

The Institute of Social Studies Trust (ISST), a non-profit research and advocacy organization based in New Delhi, India, initiated the project and housed the DAWN Secretariat until 1986, when it was relocated to the Instituto Universitário de Pesquisas do Rio de Janeiro (IUPERJ), a Brazilian graduate school and social science research institute. Institutions which lent support during the first stage of the project are the Women and Development Unit of the University of the West Indies (WAND), the Association of African Women for Research and Development (AAWORD), and the Christian Michelsen Institute (CMI). The Asian and Pacific Development Center (APDC), the Pacific and Asian Women's Forum (PAWF), the Asian Women's Research and Action Network (AWRAN), the IUPERJ, and El Colegio de Mexico participated enthusiastically. In addition, the following groups and institutions encouraged the nurturance and development of DAWN's activities. The U.N. Institute for Training and Research for the Advancement of Women (Santo Domingo), the Indian Council of Social Science Research, the International Council for Anthropological and Ethnological Sciences, the Indian Association of Women's Studies, Economists Interested in Women's Issues Group (India), the Centre for Women's Development Studies (New Delhi), the International Women's Tribune Center (New York), ISIS International (Rome and Santiago), the International Center for Research on Women (Washington, D.C.), the Mediterranean Women's Studies Institute (Athens), the Carlos Chagas Foundation (São Paulo), Centro de la Mujer Peruana Flora Tristán (Lima), the Federación de la Mujer Cubana (Havana), the Brazilian Women's Rights Council (São Paulo), the Arab Women's Studies Association (Beirut), Women and Development Consultancy Services, Ltd. (Nairobi), the Institute for Social Studies (The Hague), and Kali for Women (New Delhi).

Funding for the first phase of DAWN's activities was provided by the Ford Foundation, the Norwegian Agency for International Development (NORAD), the Swedish Agency for Research Cooperation with Developing Countries (SAREC), the Finnish International Development Agency (FINIDA), and the NGO Forum Secretariat. The Population Council supplied office space and support services during the writing of this book, which was first published in English by the Christian Michelson Institute in Bergen, Norway, in 1985. To that text, we have now added a new Preamble and Introduction.

Special thanks are also due to those who made invaluable individual contributions to DAWN's first three Advisory Committee meetings. There are many other organizations and individuals who believe in the aims of this project and who have come to view it as their own. They are so numerous that it is not possible to acknowledge them except in this collective manner. Their generous commitments of time and energy will continue to sustain this process and help to realize the visions set forth in this book.

—Bangalore, India
September 1986

Introduction

The major issues of development, social and economic crisis, the subordination of women, and feminism may appear to some as too wide-ranging and disparate to be understood within one coherent and unified framework. Yet these issues are more closely related than academic and institutional discussions would suggest. In this book we begin to clarify for ourselves the nature of these relationships and to explore their meanings for those involved in policy and practical action. We hope this analytic base can serve as a catalyst for further discussion, policy change, and experimentation aimed at fundamental improvement in the status of women, and hence their families, communities, and societies.

Our knowledge of women's experiences with the development process – as researchers, activists, and policymakers – has brought us to a range of common understandings despite different starting points. The United Nations Decade for the Advancement of Women (1975–1985) made many of these experiences possible, prodding virtually every development body – United Nations agencies, national governments, and private organizations – to develop projects and programs that would improve the economic and social position of women. The implicit assumption behind many of these programs was that women's main problem in the Third World was insufficient participation in an otherwise benevolent process of growth and development. Increasing women's participation and improving their shares in resources, land, employment, and income relative to men were seen as both necessary and sufficient to effect dramatic improvements in their living conditions.

A critical examination of the large volume of empirical evidence amassed throughout the U.N. Decade, as well as our own experiences as researchers and activists, now lead us to challenge these assumptions.[1] These studies show that rather than improving, the socioeconomic status of the great majority of Third World women has worsened considerably throughout the Decade. With few exceptions, women's relative access to economic resources, income, and employment has worsened, their burdens of work have increased, and their relative and even absolute health, nutritional, and educational status has declined. The limited success of the integrationist approach is due in part to the difficulties of overcoming traditional cultural attitudes and prejudices regarding women's participation in economic and social life. However, an equally important but mostly overlooked factor is the nature of the development process into which women were to be integrated.

In Chapter 1, we will examine in greater depth why and how strategies designed to achieve overall economic growth and increase agricultural and industrial productivity have proven to be inimical to women. We will argue that fundamental conflicts have arisen between women's economic well-being and wider development plans and processes. Such conflicts occur both because gender relations oppress women and because many long-term economic processes have been harmful – or at best indifferent – to the interests and needs of poor people in general. We will examine in greater detail how the emphasis on private property and commercialization has often reduced women's access to resources, and how the marginalization of basic needs from the dominant production structures has downgraded their own role as the predominant fulfillers of those needs.

During the past decade, a series of interlinked crises of massive and growing impoverishment, food insecurity and non-availability, financial and monetary disarray, environmental degradation, and growing demographic pressure have worsened the problem. The majority of the world's population finds it increasingly difficult to fulfill even the basic requirements of life and to survive from one day to the next. Rather than channeling available resources into programs aimed at eliminating poverty and the burden of gender and other forms of subordination, nations and the international polity have tended to react to these pressures through increased militarization, domestic repression, and foreign aggression. In donor and agency circles, there is a growing sense of hopelessness, even lack of concern, about the Third World's poor. This is compounded by the shift to bilateralism in aid and loans and cutbacks in contributions to multilateral institutions by some of the richest, most powerful, and most militaristic nations. As a result, Third World nations are increasingly being forced to rely on internal resource mobilization to make up for sharp reductions in the availability of external resources.

These problems in the world economy now present serious difficulties for the body of economic development theory. Development models as such took shape during the reconstruction efforts of southern and southeastern Europe in the aftermath of World War II. They gained considerable richness as they were elaborated during the following decades to provide analytical frameworks for the efforts made by the newly independent states of the Third World to hasten the pace of economic growth, to build social infrastructure, and to improve the living standards of their people. In each region, important schools of thought have now developed models appropriate to the specific conditions of Third World economies and cultures. It would take us too far afield to discuss the debates and changes in analytical fashions that development analysis has undergone. However, insofar as the impact of development processes on the well-being of the broad mass of people is concerned, the 1970s witnessed a general shift in development theory from the earlier belief that rapid economic growth would automatically "trickle down" in the form of improved living standards to the poorer sections of the population. (Of course, not all development models have been premised on such a belief; we are referring here to the mainstream of Anglo-American theory.) In the face of considerable evidence that economic growth does not "trickle down," in the manner expected, international development agencies came to accept the need to provide directly for the basic needs of the majority of Third World people. But even as this strategic understanding began to take hold, the economic uncertainties, upheavals, and inflationary recession of the past decade began to shake the foundations of development analysis and macro-economic theory in general. Agencies like the World Bank have responded by de-emphasizing basic needs and espousing models of structural adjustment.

As Chapter 2 will explain, the implementation of such programs has had a devastating effect on poor people in the Third World. We do not propose in this book a full-blown alternative analytic model to structural adjustment, but we do wish to argue that, when we start from the perspective of poor Third World women, we give a much needed reorientation to development analysis. This perspective emphasizes critical dimensions of resource use and abuse – a central issue for all economic theory. It focuses attention once again on the related problems of poverty and inequality, and forces recognition of forgotten sections of the population, those who are usually relegated to the status of second-class citizens. Perhaps most importantly, it points out how the empowerment of women can provide new possibilities for moving beyond current economic dilemmas.

As we will show in Chapter 3, women's contributions – as workers and as managers of human welfare – are central to the ability of households, communities, and nations to tackle the current crisis of survival. Even as resources to strengthen poor women's economic opportunities are shrinking, women have begun to mobilize themselves, both individually and collectively, in creative ways. It is only by reinforcing and building upon their efforts in such vital sectors as food production, commerce, and trade that the needed long-term transformation to more self-reliant national development strategies can be achieved. Thus, while the poor and the middle-income earners may face serious and immediate hardships, the solutions developed to address these crises may lead to policies that are more geared to meeting survival and subsistence needs.

As part of this process of empowerment, we need to reaffirm and clarify our understanding of feminism. Over the past twenty years the women's movement has debated the links between the eradication of gender subordination and of other forms of social and economic oppression based on nation, class, or ethnicity. We strongly support the position in this debate that feminism cannot be monolithic in its issues, goals, and strategies, since it constitutes the political expression of the concerns and interests of women from different regions, classes, nationalities, and ethnic backgrounds. While gender subordination has universal elements, feminism cannot be based on a rigid concept of universality that negates the wide variation in women's experience. There is and must be a diversity of feminisms, responsive to the different needs and concerns of different women, and *defined by them for themselves*. This diversity builds on a common opposition to gender oppression and hierarchy, but this is only the first step in articulating and acting upon a political agenda.

This heterogeneity gives feminism its dynamism and makes it the most potentially powerful challenge to the status quo. It allows the struggle against subordination to be waged in all arenas – from relations in the home to relations between nations – and it necessitates substantial change in cultural, economic, and political formations.[2]

For many women, problems of nationality, class, and race are inextricably linked to their specific oppression as women. Defining feminism to include the struggle against all forms of oppression is both legitimate and necessary. In many instances gender equality must be accompanied by changes on these other fronts. But at the same time, the struggle against gender subordination cannot be compromised during the struggle against other forms of oppression, or be relegated to a future when they may be wiped out.

Many Third World[3] women are acutely conscious of the need for this clarification and self-affirmation. Throughout the Decade they have faced accusations from two sides: from those who dismiss them as not being truly "feminist" because of their unwillingness to separate the struggle against gender subordination from that against other oppressions, and from those who accuse them of dividing class or national struggles and sometimes of uncritically following women's liberation movements imported from outside. This is why we strongly affirm that feminism strives for the broadest and deepest development of society and human beings free of *all* systems of domination. Such a global vision has been articulated before, particularly at strategy sessions in Bangkok in 1979 and at Stony Point, New York, in 1980.[4a] This book builds on those earlier initiatives, sharpens our analysis, and strengthens our attempts at change. While we refer to this as a "Third World" perspective, it includes all those who share our vision: from the South countries, from oppressed and disadvantaged groups and sectors of the women's movement within the North, and all others who are committed to working toward its fulfillment.

In this context, we believe that it is from the perspective of the most oppressed – i.e., women who suffer on account of class, race, and nationality – that we can most clearly grasp the nature of the links in the chain of oppression and explore the kinds of actions that we must now take. Such a perspective implies that a development process that shrinks and poisons the pie available to poor people, and then leaves women scrambling for a larger relative share, is not in women's interest. We reject the belief that it is possible to obtain sustainable improvements in women's economic and social position under conditions of growing relative inequality, if not absolute poverty, for both women and men.[4] Equality for women is impossible within the existing economic, political, and cultural processes that reserve resources, power, and control for small groups of people. But neither is development possible without greater equity for, and participation by, women.

Our vision of feminism has at its very core a process of economic and social development geared to human needs through wider control over and access to economic and political power. The substance of this book evolved out of the experience of women who have attempted in practical and analytical ways to come to grips with the implications of such a vision. Our purpose was not to expand or present new data or research results, but rather to place the diverse body of micro-level case studies, projects, and organizing attempts in a wider and more unified context. We hope thereby, through the collective process that this book represents, to move toward a framework that can reknit the fabric of development theory and action by drawing together the strands of improved living standards, socially responsible management and use of resources, elimination of gender subordination and socioeconomic inequality, and the organizational restructuring that can bring these about.

Chapter 1 examines how women's experiences with economic growth, commercialization, and market expansion are determined by both class and gender, tracing these experiences through colonial and post-colonial times. In Chapter 2 we link the past history of development policies and strategies to the current systemic crises – in the production and distribution of food, water and fuel availability, international debt, militarization, and a growing conservatism opposed to women's changing roles. This chapter also establishes the importance of women's potential for mitigating the effects of these crises through their role in ensuring the reproduction of their families and communities. In writing this chapter, it became apparent that there is a dearth of material that illuminates the specific sectoral effects of the food, energy, and debt crises and examines their interconnections. Only recently are efforts underway to collect evidence, document the impact by class and gender, and analyze the results within a global framework. Research in this area constitutes a central focus of DAWN's ongoing activities.

Finally, Chapter 3 seeks to broaden the dialogue on the strategies and methods that women need to overcome these crises and move toward a society in which women and men participate equally with justice and dignity. As we noted earlier, the discussion in this chapter is tentative and in need of elaboration through continuous discussion within the women's movement, but it nevertheless suggests some of the long- and short-term policy changes and strategies consonant with a feminist vision of a better society. Because women's organizations are central to these strategies, the chapter also evaluates the strengths and weaknesses of different types of organizations and suggests the changes needed to make them more effective in shaping and pressuring for a new policy agenda.

Our main audience for this book is women. Indeed, the actions undertaken by women individually and through organizations have been the most exciting and potentially most promising events of the last decade. Women have come together in organizations, networks, and movements. They have tackled problems of income and employment, and altered the ways in which society, governments, international institutions, men, and they themselves evaluate their own work. They have struggled to bring the issues of basic human survival and the right to live in dignity to the forefront of public consciousness, to organize against military repression and militarization, and to mobilize their energies in a host of other ways. Women, therefore, have been the catalysts behind many of the actions of governments, agencies, and others during the last ten years.

It is important for us in the women's movement to understand

and acknowledge our own achievements and strengths. In 1986, the ideological climate and mood are gloomier regarding the prospects for peace and genuine human and economic development than they were at the beginning of the 1970s. It is easy to be discouraged about the concrete improvements in women's economic and social position, which appear to have been as meagre as the resources that agencies and governments have actually directed to women. But let us look at our experiences in another way. We know now from our own research that the subordination of women has a long history and is deeply ingrained in economic, political, and cultural processes. What we have managed to do in the last few years is to forge grassroots women's movements and worldwide networks such as never existed before, to begin to transform that subordination and in the process to break down other oppressive structures as well. Women know all too well how hard they have had to struggle in their families, political organizations, and communities to achieve the personal autonomy that fuels and builds upon wider socioeconomic change. Initially equipped with little knowledge or preparation to challenge the full weight of gender oppression (intertwined as it is with class, national, and ethnic subordination), we have acquired skills, self-confidence, and the capacity to organize for change.

While it is principally to such a process of ongoing empowerment of women that this book is dedicated, many of the issues, the analysis, and the strategies proposed are also addressed to governments and agencies. But we have learned from our experiences of the past decade that the political will for serious action by those in power is contingent on women organizing to demand and promote change. We therefore need to assert our claim in shaping the major social and economic issues facing our times. In order to clarify the role that we can play in coming years, the successes, failures, and potential of our organizations must be assessed. We do this with the recognition that few contemporary social movements have the mass potential, the freshness of vision, the courage to experiment with new methods for action, and the respect for diversity and challenge of the women's movement. It is time for us to assert this with clarity, rigor, and passion.

—September 1986

// 1 //

Gender and Class in Development Experience

From the Vantage Point of Poor Women

The development debates of the last three decades have generally been conducted from the vantage points of different protagonists. The competing positions taken on such key issues as growth versus people-centred development, export-led growth versus inward-oriented production, the problems of international money and finance, the proper role and functioning of multinational corporations, and on technological modernization and appropriateness, all reflect the interests and concerns of various agents in the processes of economic and social transformation. Such actors usually include: different, and sometimes conflicting, national or regional interests; transnational or domestic firms; different groups of peasants, agricultural or industrial workers; and the landless or the unemployed. It is only within the last decade that a new protagonist has come to be recognized– women from the poorest, most oppressed sections of all societies.

The perspective of poor and oppressed women provides a unique and powerful vantage point from which we can examine the effects of development programmes and strategies. This point of departure is fruitful for a number of reasons. *First*, if the goals of development include improved standards of living, removal of poverty, access to dignified employment, and reduction in societal inequality, then it is quite natural to start with women. They constitute the majority of the poor, the underemployed, and the economically and socially disadvantaged in most societies. Furthermore, women suffer from the additional burdens imposed by gender-based hierarchies and subordination.

Second, women's work, underremunerated and undervalued as it is, is vital to the survival and ongoing reproduction of human beings in all societies. In food production and processing, in responsibility for fuel, water, health care, child-rearing, sanitation, and the entire range of so-called basic needs, women's labour is dominant. Thus, if we are to understand the impact of development strategies on these same needs, the viewpoint of women as the principal producers and workers is an obvious starting point.

Third, in many societies women's work in trade, services and traditional industries is widespread. And finally, it is now recognized that women workers are often predominant in the most technologically advanced industries such as electronics, as well as in export production. The impact of development on technology, employment, incomes, and working conditions in these sectors is of interest not only to the women who work in them, but also to the economies dependent on the employment, foreign exchange earnings, or incomes thereby generated.

The vantage point of poor women thus enables us not only to evaluate the extent to which development strategies benefit or harm the poorest and most oppressed sections of the people, but also to judge their impact on a range of sectors and activities crucial to socioeconomic development and human welfare. But before we develop this perspective, a number of caveats are in order. Although we focus on poor women as the starting point for understanding development, our vision, strategies, and methods are addressed to all women. We hope this analysis can contribute to the ongoing debate about the commonalities and differences in the oppression of women of different nations, classes, or ethnic groups. "Sisterhood" is not an abstract principle; it is a concrete goal that must be achieved through a process of debate and action.

Another qualifier is that while most of our examples of development's impact are drawn from the Third World, we believe that many of the issues raised – including the very meaning of development itself – are equally relevant to the more industrialized countries. Perhaps because the Western feminist movement (especially in the U.S.) gained strength in the late 1960s and early 1970s during most of which time employment, social services, and incomes (at least of the white majority) were relatively insulated from the shocks of the world economy, gaining parity with men often took the centre stage for the mainstream of the movement. But even during that time, the dissonant voices of poor women from racially or nationally oppressed groups could be heard stating their priorities – food, housing, jobs, services, and the struggle against racism. Equality with men who themselves suffered unemployment, low wages, poor work conditions and racism within the existing socioeconomic structures did not seem an adequate or worthy goal. Many white and middle-class women also held this view, both in the U.S. and a number of European countries. But it was not until the overt attacks on employment and social services began in the mid-1970s that the mainstream of the white women's movement awoke to the "feminization of poverty." A significant literature now exists on this and on the implications of newly emerging technologies, and we draw on it later.

A third major caveat is that we do not address the experience of socialist countries. Although this experience represents significantly different development strategies, and although some literature exists on the particular experiences of women under socialism, limitations of time and space have prevented us from discussing it here. We hope that our resultant sharper focus on the development experiences of women in non-socialist Third World countries will better enable us to understand the concrete problems faced by societies in a transition to socialism, as well as its alternative visions and potentials. A careful reading of the historical experience of socialist societies indicates that they better satisfy many of the basic requirements of human life, and they tend to draw women into nontraditional production. However, the structures of gender subordination within families, social consciousness, and the political leadership have proven remarkably stubborn. As a result, a conscious attempt to break down these structures is essential, and women's organizations have often played a critical role. It is important for us to evaluate these experiences within their social, economic, and historical milieus, rather than on the basis of some theoretical ideal type of socialism. This evaluation can best be grounded in concrete realities through the participation of women from socialist countries. We hope in the next stage of our work to begin such a discussion.

The main theme of this chapter is that women's experiences with processes of economic growth, commercialization, and market expansion are determined by both gender and class. Existing economic and political structures tend to be highly inequitable between nations, classes, genders, and ethnic groups. These structures are often the historical legacy of colonial domination. We argue, however, that post-colonial development processes and strategies have often exacerbated these inequities, and in some instances even worsened the levels of absolute poverty. The interests of powerful nations and classes, both internationally and nationally, are enmeshed in these structures, and therefore often have a vested interest in their persistence. As a result, the survival of large sections of the population in the Third World has become increasingly uncertain and vulnerable.

For women this vulnerability is further reinforced by systems of male domination that, on the one hand, deny or limit their access to economic resources and political participation, and on the other hand, impose sexual divisions of labour that allocate to them the most onerous, labour-intensive, poorly rewarded tasks inside and outside the home, as well as the longest hours of work. Thus when development programmes have negative effects, these are felt more acutely by women.

Traditional gender-based subordination has typically limited women's access to and control over such productive resources as land and labour, imposed sexual divisions of labour (in which women's work is accorded lower status or social importance), and curtailed women's physical mobility. Of course, the specifics of subordination vary considerably across regions, historical time periods, and classes. A considerable amount of the research conducted before and during the past decade addresses precisely these variations, and there is now available a wealth of analysis rich in sectoral, regional, countrywide, and sub-national detail. For example, while women of both the propertied and the working classes are subordinate to men, the nature of that subordination differs considerably. For poor women it may take the form of longer and harder work, while for richer women it may appear as controls on physical mobility and sexuality.

Gender-based subordination is deeply ingrained in the consciousness of both men and women and is usually viewed as a natural corollary of the biological differences between them. It is reinforced through religious beliefs, cultural practices, and educational systems (both traditional and modern) that assign to women lesser status and power. This takes a number of forms. The sexual division of labour is not only viewed as naturally given, but "women's work" is considered demeaning to men and their manhood if they perform it. It is usually seen as male prerogative to be personally served by women within the home. As is now well-known, with very few exceptions, the spheres of religion and politics have been dominated and controlled by men. Even though female religious rituals and practices have existed, they have generally been more confined outside mainstream religions, although here again exceptions do exist.

The threat of sexual violence to restrict women's physical mobility and to punish women who flouted social norms was practiced in most societies. Rape and other forms of sexual abuse are not individual acts; they have often received social sanction. And even when they have not, the victim is usually blamed for the aggressor's action. Forms of sexual mutilation have been traditionally practiced to ensure male control of female sexuality, sometimes as part of the system of male monopoly over property and inheritance. That older women themselves are often in charge of mutilations should not make us overlook the fact that it is the underlying structure of male power over women's lives that sanctions, indeed enforces, such practices. The resulting psychological trauma wrought on women and girls is manifest in their own belief that those who do not undergo the mutilations are unclean and impure.[5]

The control of women through sexual violence for reasons of property and inheritance is only one aspect. In many societies public spaces are physically dominated by men, making it extremely difficult for women to move, work, or earn a livelihood within them. (Women, however, do defy this norm.) This operates against women of all classes, though perhaps not in identical ways. Sexual control over women adds one more barrier to their ability to perform wage labour, market products, or obtain access to necessary services. Men are often oblivious of the extent to which fears of sexual aggression manipulate and threaten women's lives.[6]

As we know, women have been the butt of male ridicule in proverbs and myths throughout history. While women have sometimes responded in kind, the predominant myths are usually insulting to women's bodies, mental capacities, and social behaviour. Modern education and mass media often perpetuate such sex-biased stereotypes. It is only with the growth of the women's movement that these prejudices have been challenged in any coherent way. Thus the cultural subordination of women has reinforced male control of resources and power, and the divisions of labour that have enshrined male privileges

While traditional gender based systems of subordination have been considerably transformed by the forces of economic growth, commercialization, and market expansion, subordination itself persists, although in some cases more impersonal forces in the labour market replace the direct control of women within patriarchal rural households.[7] We must understand the impact of these processes on women's relative access to resources, income and employment, as well as on the sexual division of labour. The combined effects are then reflected in women's health and nutritional status, access to education, ability to control biological reproduction, and, perhaps most important, in women's autonomy. The almost uniform conclusion of the Decade's research is that, with a few exceptions, women's relative access to economic resources, incomes, and employment has worsened, their burdens of work have increased, and their relative and even absolute health, nutritional, and educational status has declined.[8] A clearer understanding of the causes must be sought initially in those larger development processes which affect poor women.

The Colonial Heritage

Variations in economic structures, political institutions, and cultural milieus notwithstanding, and despite considerable differences in the rates of economic accumulation and growth especially in the last fifteen to twenty years, most of the countries of the Third World exhibit remarkably little divergence in the patterns and consequences of development. At most, a small spectrum of patterns and processes can be identified along which band most Third World countries lie. These include:

- an unfavourable structural location in the international economy,
- vulnerability to the cycles and vagaries of international trade, prices, and capital flows,
- profound internal inequalities of land ownership and control over resources, access to income and employment,
- deprivation of such basic needs as adequate nutrition, health,

housing, water, energy, sanitation, and education to significant sections of the population.

As scholars and analysts now recognize, these problems are in part the legacy of colonial systems of surplus transfer out of the Third World. But their persistence well into the third U.N. Development Decade bespeaks powerful underlying structures that have not been significantly modified. While not every Third World country suffers from all of the problems noted above, all experience at least one or more of them.

The structural features resulting from the Third World countries' location in the international economy have been the subject of an extensive literature and debate.[9] To summarize, both during the colonial era, and under new forms in the post-colonial period, the economic relations between developing countries and developed countries have tended to operate against the interests of the former so as to increase their vulnerability to exernal events and pressures. As is now widely recognized, the economic and political structures of colonial rule converted subject territories into sources of cheap raw materials, food, and labour, and markets for the ruling countries' manufactures. The system operated not only to drain resources and wealth away from the colonies; it created export enclaves in agriculture, mining, and other primary sub-sectors, and transformed self-provisioning communities through forced commercialization and the introduction of private property in land. Colonial control suppressed the manufacturing potential of the colonies and destroyed traditional crafts and artisan production through imports of manufactures.[10]

The specific pattern varied from country to country, as did the extent of the resulting impoverishment of the population, the exacerbation of inequalities in access to land, resources, and power, and the growth of powerful internal classes and groups whose interests were linked to the maintenance of an open economy. That large sections of the people were severely impoverished, and that the seeds of environmental degradation, demographic pressure, and land misuse were planted during the colonial era is well enough known. These facts bear repetition, however, because therein lies the genesis of the current crisis of survival that afflicts Third World populations, and women in particular.

For example, in areas of southern and eastern Africa the bulk of the land was taken over by settlers while the indigenous populations were forced onto small tracts of poor quality land, inherently incapable of sustaining the intensive agricultural practices forced by the resulting population densities. In Latin America and the Caribbean the decimation of indigenous populations was followed by the absorption of land into large landed estates serviced by cheap slave labour or small tenants often under debt peonage. Enclave plantations producing such profitable export crops as coffee, sugar, tobacco, cotton, tea, and jute sprang into existence in most regions of the Third World, along with mines for copper, bauxite, and other raw materials. In parts of South and Southeast Asia, although the bulk of the land remained in local hands, systems of private property were introduced to facilitate the extraction of land revenues and other taxes by the colonial authority. Forced cultivation of export commodities such as indigo or cotton has been extensively documented.[11]

The colonial era thus laid the basis for the particular position of Third World countries in the world economy. Primary exports became the most important growth pole in most countries, complemented by a weak industrial sector. Alienation of large segments of the population from the land or their access to land under highly exploitative conditions, degradation of forests and soils, the resulting pressure on resources, and the rapid growth of urban slums, all testify to the impoverishment experienced by the majority of the Third World's people during the colonial period.

Women's experiences of the colonial era have now been documented, although considerable research still remains to be done.[12] The growth of female poverty under colonial rule was noted early on by Ester Boserup who pointed out that colonial rulers tended to disfavour women in access to land, technology, and employment.[13] However, the patriarchal ideology of the colonialists was only partly responsible for the worsening of women's economic position. The inherent inequality and poverty-creating character of economic and political processes was an equally important factor. While large numbers of both women and men were impoverished by these processes, women tended to suffer more. When private property in land was introduced, for example, women more often than men lost traditional land use-rights. It was women's labour that tended to be unpaid and ill-specified under systems of tenancy and debt peonage. When traditional manufactures decayed, it was often female employment and incomes that were affected most, as for example in food processing. Women were often left with meagre resources to feed and care for children, the aged, and the infirm when men migrated or were conscripted into forced labour by the colonialists. In areas where slavery had been extensive, racism added a third oppression to those of gender and class.[14] It must be remembered that colonial rule tended to be inherently racist even without the presence of slavery. The effect of colonial racism on gender hierarchy has been studied very little outside the regions where slavery prevailed.

Resource Inequalities
and "Open" Economic Policies

In the previous section we traced two broad types of effects of colonial rule on Third World countries. On the one hand, it introduced private property, commercial production and export orientation, and geared production in agriculture, industry, services, and trade to the above. On the other hand, and as a result, large sections of the population were alienated from adequate or stable resources, income, or employment. In particular, the basic needs of food, health, housing, and the like became increasingly marginal to the main orientation of the production structures. These two trends had very specific consequences for women. Private property and commercializaton often reduced their access to resources, even more so than men. The marginalization of the basic requirements of decent life downgraded their own role as the predominant fulfillers of those needs. We pick up these trends in our analysis of the post-colonial era.

Given the fact that the colonial period created and accentuated inequalities both *among* nations, and between classes and genders (also castes, ethnic communities, races, etc.) *within* nations, it would have taken a considerable reorientation of political and economic structures following independence to effect significant changes. Indeed, major structural shifts have occurred, creating industrial booms and rapid growth in some countries, especially between the mid-1960s and mid 1970s, and widening the gap among Third World countries themselves.[15] Yet, for most countries there has been little structural realignment. With some exceptions among the so-called "newly industrializing countries" (NICs), most Third World countries have retained many of the dominant features of the colonial era. Primary export enclaves persist; continued concentration on traditional exports has been justified on the grounds of comparative cost advantages.[16] There has been little substantial growth of the manufacturing sector except in the handful of NICs and a few other large countries such as India.[17]

The dualism in agriculture has taken on new forms. The colonial combination of dynamic export agriculture with stagnating subsistence production has turned into a combination of prosperous commercial agriculture with a marginalized semi-proletariat that can neither subsist off its own landholding nor find adequate employment as a substitute. This is the case in the Philippines, for example, where fruit cultivation under multinational auspices has taken place at the expense of food production.[18] Even in a NIC like Mexico, strawberries are produced for export in the Northwest while the impoverished communal farms cannot generate an adequate subsistence.[19] In Central America cattle ranching and appropriation of the most fertile lands by crops such as cotton, coffee, and sugar cane have deprived peasant communities of land on a large scale.[20]

In both the agricultural and industrial sectors, as well as in tertiary activities such as tourism and trade, effective control over production, allocation, and distribution decisions is often in the hands of multinational corporations that subordinate national interests to their own global profit and growth strategies.[21] In Third World countries multinationals not only obtain generous terms for producing in free trade zones, they generally evade responsibility for environmental and health hazards.[22] Further, employment creation is slow since the pressures of international competition tend to dictate the use of capital-intensive production methods.

From a policy or action perspective it is important to understand the underlying economic processes and development strategies that have created or accentuated the structural features outlined above. Central among these is the gearing of development strategies to satisfy the requirements of an economy open to the flows of foreign private capital and the expansion of the foreign trade sector. The full weight of orthodox economic analysis has been brought to bear on the propositions that free trade and free capital flows lead to an optimal allocation of scarce resources to the mutual benefit of all countries.[23] Indeed, export-based industrialization has been championed as leading to greater production efficiency because of the pressures of international competition.

Without ignoring the problems and weaknesses of countries' experiences with import-substituting industrialization, it is important to assign blame and credit where due. While inward-oriented development strategies are routinely criticized for excessive bureaucratic controls and managerial/administrative waste, misallocation and corruption,[24] it must be acknowledged that most countries suffering from these problems have not pursued inward-oriented strategies at all! Second, while a number of countries have been following "open," export-oriented strategies for a number of years, only a few have gained systematic results. A number of NICs have experienced growth booms, but these have been accompanied by worsening or at best unchanged income inequalities as well as structural and regional dualisms and disarticulation.[25] Brazil is a case in point, where the economic boom of 1967–73 went hand in hand with sharply growing inequalities.[26] Further, as the late 1970s and 1980s have shown, the growth in these countries, based on external private capital flows, is no longer sustainable due to balance of payments crises and the pressures of debt repayment.[27] Third, those East Asian countries (South Korea, Taiwan) which have had particular successes in growth, employment generation, and increased real income for large sections of the population (although under repressive political regimes) had prior successful redistributive *agrarian reforms* as a key ingredient both in generating the incomes and the demand needed for a growing *internal* market for industry, and in reducing income inequalities.[28]

It appears doubtful, therefore, whether single minded devotion to either export promotion or laissez-faire will dramatically alter the economic structure of Third World countries. The Chilean economic debacle under monetarist and "supply-side" policies after 1973 has been amply documented.[29] Rather, what is required are direct structural changes through thoroughgoing land reforms and an evening out of inequalities in wealth and income. This would serve to release the productive potential of agriculture in line with the needs of internal consumption, and to create the incomes and demand to sustain the internal market for manufactures.[30] Our argument is therefore not against export expansion per se. *Rather, we argue that export promotion under conditions of extreme inequalities of land holding and income will not create the needed backward linkages to domestic production, and will probably worsen existing inequalities.*

Even in sub-Saharan Africa, where landholding inequalities are not as severe as in Latin America, or where absolute landlessness is not as problematic as in Asia, the diversion of resources to export crops has reduced land available for food production, increased the pressure on fragile eco-agricultural systems, and contributed to the slow growth of food production.[31] While declarations in favour of self-reliance in food production, technology, etc. have been made time and time again,[32] few governments have been able effectively to counter either the internal pressures from those groups who stand to gain from the "open" economy, or the external pressures from bilateral aid donors, multilateral institutions, or transnational corporations.[33] During the last decade more and more countries have turned to an outward-looking economic strategy. Indeed, under the pressures of world recession and slowdowns in trade, Third World countries are under greater pressure than ever to open their economies to foreign capital and to divert resources to exports.[34]

We now turn to the sectoral effects of this orientation of the production structure from the perspective of poor, working women. In rural areas women's access to land, labour, technology, credit, and other inputs into cultivation appears to have worsened in most parts of the Third World.[35] When land reforms have been undertaken, they have often *reduced* women's control over land by ignoring their traditional use-rights and giving land titles solely to male heads of households.[36] Landless women from the poorest households are more likely to predominate as seasonal, casual, and temporary labourers at lower wages than their male counterparts.[37] Where agricultural mechanization has occurred, it worsens or at best does not improve women's absolute and relative economic position.[38] Mechanization of food-processing technologies often drastically reduces women's employment and income.[39] In some cases, even the general premise that women and men will be affected in the same direction by processes of commercialization cannot be upheld. In parts of West Africa the introduction of cash crops has improved the economic position of some men but worsened the income and work status of women from the same households.[40] Women's workloads in tasks such as fuel gathering and water collection have in fact tended to increase with "development" in many instances, as waste and common lands have been privatized, and traditional tree cover has been exploited for commercial purposes.[41]

In the industrial sector the picture is more mixed, since the employment of Third World women in certain export-based industries and occupations has in fact been increasing.[42] These growth industries are typically consumer electronics, semi-conductors, toys and sporting goods, textiles and apparel, footwear and luggage, wigs, optical equipment, and bicycles.[43] However, within these industries women tend to be segregated into a relatively narrow range of occupations which they dominate. Wages in these industries (often located in free trade zones under multinational auspices) vary widely among countries, which accounts for the constant shifting of firms from one location to another. Furthermore, employment in these industries tends to be short-term with high turnover, leaving the women little choice but to move into sweatshop occupations or the so-called "informal" sector once they lose their jobs.[44] It must also be stressed that in comparison to the absolute size of the female population or workforce in developing countries, the recent increase in women's industrial employment is small.[45]

It is of course true that, especially in the short run, individual women from poor households are in such urgent need of income that they must take any employment they can get. Indeed, factory employment in exporting firms may often be a better alternative to other work that is available to women, even if it is only for a short duration. Attempts to improve the income and working conditions in this sector pose a serious dilemma. Since multinational corporations locate in these countries principally because of the presence of cheap female labour, attempts to demand better wages, working conditions, job security, and advancement prospects often induce further capital flight. This problem requires much deeper discussion than it has received thus far.

A related issue is that we must improve our ability to anticipate the impact of the newly emerging technologies on women in both the industrial countries and the Third World. This is a major area for combined research and action by women from these different regions. The shift of women workers away from traditional occupations to areas where they will learn new skills is one way of reducing their vulnerability to technological, social and industrial changes. The sector of office work, in which a technological revolution is taking place through the use of computers, microelectronics and word processors, is an important case where, given existing gender hierarchies, women are generally being confined to operator status at low pay and poor working conditions.

More common loci of women's manufacturing employment are in traditional crafts, in the "informal" sector, in export handicrafts, and in certain modern industries such as textile factories or agro-processing. Often women work as unpaid family workers in home-based putting-out systems under extremely exploitative conditions of wages and work.[46] As employees in the small-scale export sector, they often experience a type of labour control that is almost feudal in its requirements of subservience and dependence. While women's employment in the exports sector (either in free trade zones, in small shops, or home-based putting-out work) has been growing, their employment in traditional crafts has been declining as these crafts are themselves dying out, and their employment in factories producing for the internal market tends to stagnate in most countries.[47] Women remain the most poorly paid, badly organized, and vulnerable group of industrial workers in the Third World and elsewhere, and the record of trade unions in this regard continues to be a sorry one.

Apart from the above, women are found in disproportionate numbers in petty trade, commerce, and services.[48] While in some instances women's presence in these sectors dates back to colonial or even precolonial times, it is now often a response to economic pressure and to their lack of access to employment in agriculture or industry. There has been considerable discussion about the precise meaning and economic significance to be attached to the "informal-sector."[49] In particular, the term has been used to cover a wide range of income-generating activities, the common features of which are low wages or incomes, uncertain employment, and poor working conditions. In a Third World country such activities may include declining handicrafts, home-based production, small-scale retail trade, petty food production and other services catering to urban workers, and domestic service.

Obviously, the factors affecting the expansion or decline of employment in this sector may be quite different. Although some have argued that these activities, especially urban services, act as a reservoir for surplus labourers who gradually move up into more "formal" employment, few of them actually allow for such mobility. Further, there is considerable gender specificity to whatever mobility may exist.[50] Women are much less likely than men to move out of "informal" occupations, partly because they tend to be at the lower end of even the "informal" spectrum and hence cannot accumulate the skills, networks, or cash reserves necessary to move out; and partly because the barriers erected by sexist ideology to their entry into better occupations tend to be quite formidable.

Nevertheless, some of the most successful organizing efforts have flowered among poor, self-employed women. Examples of collective self-empowerment such as the Self-Employed Women's Association, SEWA (Ahmedabad), the Working Women's Forum (Madras), Rose Hall (St. Vincent), and a host of others testify to the fact that with some intermediary effort poor women can learn to organize themselves collectively to great effect.[51] This runs counter to the myth prevalent in trade unions and bureaucratic circles that women are inherently more conservative in their consciousness, and hence more difficult to organize. It is the male family and union members who tend to be more conservative and concerned about their own privileges when the subject of women's participation in collective organizations is raised.[52]

Not only do women constitute a larger share relative to men in "informal" activities than they do in more "formal" employment, but such activities also account for a large proportion of total female employment.[53] It is important to recognize (and not only from women's perspective) that such employment cannot in any sense be considered marginal, since it tends to account for such a significant proportion of total employment.[54] Nor is it merely a residual or declining sector. Many of its activities – particularly in urban services and trade – are a vitally important part of overall economic activity. Raising the productive capacity of this sector, and improving its working conditions, will simultaneously improve the living standards of the producers therein, as well as a large number of the urban workers and poor who consume the goods and services it creates.

Basic Needs Strategies

The recognition of the growing gap between survival needs and their fulfillment, and the failure of growth to trickle down to the poor, led in the mid-1970s to a significant shift in the stated orientation of multilateral development strategies in favour of "basic human needs." This shift was a response to estimates such as that by the Food and Agriculture Organization (FAO) in its *Fourth World Food Survey* (1977) that the number of persons in developing countries who consume less than the "critical minimum energy intake" had increased from 400 million to 450 million between 1969–71 and 1972–74. Although 1972–74 were bad years climatically in many parts of the world, and thus possibly overstated the trend increase in undernutrition, the absolute magnitudes are appalling enough. While there is considerable disagreement about the appropriateness of the different malnutrition indicators,[55] widespread malnutrition does exist, and its effects are especially acute on ,infants, growing children, and pregnant and lactating women.[56]

The "basic needs" approach as propagated by its multilateral adherents[57] emphasized the importance of project lending and granting targeted toward improvements in nutrition, health, water, sanitation, housing, and education. World Bank loans for urban "sites and services," social forestry, and improvements in the productivity of small farmers were meant to tackle the problem of widespread poverty directly or indirectly. It bears mention that this approach, espoused passionately by the Bank during the McNamara presidency, represented a repudiation of "trickle-down" theories. However, the methodology adopted for the new lending lines marked little change from the Bank's established support of commercialization and market integration and expansion. Thus, the small-farmer programmes sought to raise productivity by increasing their use of purchased inputs and credit, and by drawing

them further into the market nexus.[58] The sites and services programmes increased the rental values of urban slums and shanty
towns, and introduced private property, thereby reducing the access of the poorest to housing they could no longer afford. The
most infamous case is the Tondo project in metro-Manila.[59] Social
forestry programmes in India have come under extensive criticism
as many of them have led to the supplanting of local staple food
production by eucalyptus intended for industrial use.[60] The implications of an approach that disregards the effects of commercialization in a context of structural inequality are therefore questionable.

Apart from their emphasis on commercialization, a second crucial aspect of the new anti-poverty programmes is their singular sil-
ence on structural changes that directly address inequalities in
landholding or other resources. It is well known that in many
Third World countries, national economic plans are often no more
than a collection of bilateral and multilateral aid projects super-
vised by donor agencies. These agencies therefore exercise considerable leverage over actual economic policy, as does the International Monetary Fund (IMF) through its control of finance and the
balance of payments. Indeed, during the 1980s the World Bank
and the IMF have drawn closer together in coordinating policies
directed toward short-and long-term structural adjustment. While
this leverage has been extensively exercised to promote "openness" to private capital flows and export expansion, and to dis-
courage governmental controls over transnational corporations,[61]
it has almost never been used to promote reductions in the inequality of asset-holding.

A third aspect of these programmes is their continued use of a
top-down approach to project identification, planning and implementation.[62] Such an approach is of course not new, nor are national governments any less culpable than the multilateral institutions in this regard.[63] Indeed, the recent history of "development"
processes is replete with the struggles of the poor against policies
that reduce their access to resources, destroy and pollute their environment, or mortgage their jobs and food consumption to the requirements of debt repayments.[64] Surely those programmes meant
specifically to improve the quality of life of the poor ought to listen
to their voices.

There has been considerable discussion in development circles about the need for a "people-centred" approach to projects.[65] Such an approach should address not only projects, but the overall development policies within which they are framed. Two issues therefore become crucial. *First*, overall policies (monetary, fiscal, agricultural, industrial, social services, employment, etc.) must be *directly* oriented to meeting people's basic needs. Planning for food security, employment creation, health, literacy, etc., must not be relegated to secondary status as they too often tend to be, nor can macroeconomic policies be implemented that go against these basic needs. We of course recognize that a society may have to decide to forego present consumption in favour of investment for future consumption. But the burden of foregone consumption usually weighs most heavily and inequitably on poor people and poor nations.

The *second* crucial issue concerns the linkages between people, bureaucrats, and intermediaries (e.g. non-governmental organizations) in project choice, planning, and implementation. A typical problem at this level is that the locally powerful classes and groups tend to dominate decisions and bias them to their own interests. Replacement of local participation by bureaucratic decision making and implementation hardly improves the picture. Indeed, bureaucrats and lower-level state functionaries often side with the rich and powerful in the local community. A top-down approach wherein crucial decisions are made by bureaucrats obviates even the possibility of a local voice for the poor that may exist in local bodies.

Experience has taught us that absence of local participation in favour of a more bureaucratic approach is not only undemocratic and inequitable, but highly inefficient. The Indian experience with anti-poverty programmes (on which the government now spends almost one-sixth of public-plan outlays) run by bureaucrats in a top-down manner, is that they are poorly coordinated and tend to be insensitive both to poor people's needs and unsuited to local resources, since they are often not accountable to the local population. They are also seen as rife with corruption and considerable leakages of resources meant for the poor toward the wealthy; furthermore, they foster dependency rather than self-reliance, and they engender considerable contempt for the government mechansm.[66] Similar examples can be documented for a number of other countries as well.[67]

It is clear that it is not sufficient to focus on one or the other of these two issues. A focus on project implementation without bene-ficiary involvement in policy formulation is likely to make people's basic needs peripheral to the main thrust of policies, plans, and programmes. An emphasis on policy decisions without popular in-volvement in implementation creates bureaucratic structures that do not truly reach people at the ground level. People and basic needs must enter at both the level of overall policy decisions and the level of actual implementation.

The Development Project Experience

The criticisms of integrated projects intended to satisfy basic needs come into sharper focus when viewed from the vantage point of poor women. As an illustration of an all too typical situation, we discuss below in some detail a major project that directly addres-sed questions of food availability, health, sanitation, and employ-ment, and one in which women were indirectly integrated.

In the Kano River Project[68] major infrastructural investment led to significant changes in landholding, cropping patterns, employ-ment and consumption, as well as the environment, availability of fuel and minor produce, and the health status of the population. It also caused growing inequalities within the population as a whole and among different categories of women.

The project was a gravity-flow irrigation scheme covering some 20,000 acres of Hausaland in Northern Nigeria. The three official goals of the project were to increase local and national food sup-ply; to provide employment opportunities; and to improve the standard of living through the provision of clinics, schools, water, roads, and sanitation. Three groups of women were affected: Mus-lim women in villages, Muslim women on dispersed homesteads, and non-Muslim women.

The project design was based on the registration of all land ownership prior to irrigation, followed by the reallocation of land to the owners after the infrastructure was in place. Although pre-viously many plots were owned communally, only the "senior owners" (almost always men) were registered. The distribution

among the population was fairly arbitrary, and no attempt wa
made to reduce inequities during reallocation. Nearly one-third o
the male farmers lost almost all of their land, as did roughly th
same proportion of women farmers. Indeed, women farmers fare
somewhat worse, since even those who continued to have access t
land were now given the worst plots by their husbands. This wa
particularly true among non-Muslim women.

Increased irrigation led to greater emphasis on dry-season crops
However, increases in output were disappointing because large
scale surface irrigation worsened pest and weed problems, thu
lowering productivity. Also, the cost of inputs rose substantially
making the new crops difficult to adopt. Major differences emer
ged between the larger and better-irrigated farms and the others
Wet-season crops received fewer inputs and their output tended t
decline. As a result, the cropping pattern shifted from previou
local staples to wheat and tomatoes, but with a serious reductior
in overall crop diversity. Sorghum and millet grown by women ir
the wet season suffered the most.

The effects of the project on local food availability were mixed
Certainly the more prosperous farms improved their consumptior
standards. And, because of a failure in the project's intendec
transfer of wheat to urban bakeries, some of the wheat increase
did find their way into the local markets. Muslim village womer
were able to take advantage of this by increased processing o
wheat snack goods to meet the food demands of migrant worker
in the project area and thereby increase their own incomes. How
ever, this benefit did not accrue to non-Muslim women whose la
bour on their husband's farms increased and who lacked time, re
sources, and nearby demand for own-account activities. The over
all effect on food consumption was that it became less equal, les
varied, and less nutritious.

Although employment in the project site and on the large farm
did increase, this must be seen in the context of the growing land
lessness. Women were excluded from formal employment in pro
ject construction and administration. On the farms women tendec
to be hired as seasonal and casual labour, while men were mor
likely to obtain such permanent jobs as were available.

The project had major environmental effects. Wide-scale des
truction of forests reduced the availability of fuel and sylvan pro

duce to the poor. This inevitably increased the labour of poor women in fuel gathering. The destruction of economic trees reduced beer-brewing income, and deprived older women of income from the collection of firewood and water.

Although the project was supposed to improve health through the provision of clinics, in fact these were few, inconveniently located, and staffed only by men. Infant mortality remains high. More important, there has been a dramatic increase in diseases such as cerebral-spinal meningitis, pneumonia, and measles, as well as malaria and intestinal diseases associated with large-scale irrigation and a shift to surface sources of drinking water.

The Kano River Project is a classic example of the argument that commercialization based on unequal access to land and resources can be quite detrimental to the living standards of the poor, especially women. They lost land and sources of income, and suffered from a reduced variety of nutritious foods as well as increased drudgery. The fact that some women were able to improve their incomes because of better resources has to be set against the worsened condition of the others. Even the increased income of Muslim women was paralleled by an increase in their seclusion, although in practice they did retain some mobility.

The project design provided for little local participation and the implementation was quite insensitive to local needs, especially those of the poor. This was seen in land allocation, crop selection, and the provision of health and sanitation services. The local opposition, particularly that of women, was very vocal against such authoritarianism. We now turn to a more general discussion of the Decade's projects for women.

Ideally we would have liked to evaluate the literature on development projects in the context of an overall assessment of the socio-economic changes occurring in the project region, and in the light of larger national development processes. We would also have preferred to examine projects (including mainstream projects with no women's components, projects geared specifically to women, and those with a women's component) in terms of their effects on women's autonomy and empowerment. Although some of the newer projects are more sensitive to gender inequalities, women's work, and even questions of power and autonomy, very few pay systematic attention to the overall effects on the poor and on basic needs.

The examination of project literature proved frustrating for several reasons.[69] Project evaluations and reviews are difficult to obtain and uneven in quality. The methodology varies considerably from study to study, and most evaluations are devoid of a larger analytic framework. The earliest development projects for women were in the areas of family planning, nutrition, and maternal and child health. These projects were perceived as social welfare projects, or as "special components" that were often the first to be eliminated in the face of budgetary reductions. More recently the focus has shifted toward increasing women's productivity, either in food production and gardening, or in handicrafts or other small-scale processing activities.

The Decade's projects yielded mixed results. Many did little to change the distribution of household labour or increase women's access to resources. A number of them increased children's labour (especially that of daughters) who took on a share of the additional workload created by their mother's participation in the project. Women's incomes from project activities tended most often to stay the same or to increase slightly. In a few instances, women actually incurred debts. However, many projects also gave participants a new sense of confidence and hope for changing their situations.

A substantial proportion of all projects for women suffer from inadequate funding and managerial support. Most evaluations noted that both project and higher-level management were often not fully committed or were insensitive to changing women's situation. A second element is the dearth of financial resources for women's projects at all levels. One study of the funding practices of specialized United Nations agencies, for example, estimated that in 1982 only .05 percent of the total allocations in the United Nations system to the agricultural sector were to programmes for rural women. Moreover, it claimed that the increase in disbursements between 1974–82 was less than one-half of that for all other agricultural subsectors.[70] A survey of women's projects in other sectors funded by other donor agencies revealed that they receive dramatically less monies and attention than the larger development projects.[71]

Many donors voiced a concern about the level of funding appropriate to the absorption capacity of the implementing agency. On the one hand, women's projects can do little with limited resources (although many survive surprisingly well). This accounts in part for the marginalization of these projects, as well as the lack of success in realising their goals. On the other hand, donor evaluations have pointed out that too much funding can be as serious as too little. If the organization is small or staffed by women who are insufficiently trained in project administration, it might not have the organizational capability to absorb the additional management of expanded operations[72].

Most projects suffer from a lack of baseline information about the socioeconomic situation of project beneficiaries, and the economic requirements of the project in terms of available markets for women's products, prices of inputs, the availability of raw materials, job opportunities on completion of training programmes, and the productive potential of new crop and seed varieties under actual field conditions.[73] A recent end-of-the-Decade survey done by the United Nations Voluntary Fund for Women (U.N.V.F.W.) showed one or more of these "obstacles" to be present to some degree in a majority of women's projects in Africa, Asia, Latin America, and the Pacific.[74] Further, baseline studies do not sufficiently break down by gender and class concepts such as the household, or the farm family, or production.

Even when baseline studies have been conducted, they are often not incorporated into the initial project design. This is a serious problem, since design-stage documents release the project funds. Midcourse corrections will not make a difference if funding is not available to allocate to the women's component. In addition, women's components that are tacked on to the type of negative development projects described earlier will not offset the deleterious effects of those projects. (However, there are a small number of cases where the women's component is the only "successful" part of an otherwise poorly designed and implemented project.[75]) Despite this, we feel that poor timing is not by itself the crucial variable. Rather the issue is insufficient awareness and sensitivity of planners, inadequate financial support and staff, unrealistic timeframes for the achievement of project goals, and the lack of participation of the women beneficiaries in project design and decisions.

Some recent evaluations have begun to redress these problems.[76] Agencies have developed more uniform analytic frameworks and tools that can help monitor and review projects, raise the questions and issues necessary to educate planners, and better orient the direction of the project. One initiative in this area is the establishment of "knowledge banks" by the U.N.V.F.W. and other agencies for planners and policy makers. Checklists are another such tool, although they have limitations: they often use terminology unfamiliar to project personnel, are not uniform across projects or donor agencies, and have little institutional backup/enforcement and use. Many of these problems can be corrected with better training of project personnel, more high-level institutional support and accountability, and the increased involvement of the target population in the various decisions and stages of the project cycle.

From what we have said thus far, it is clear that there have been basic flaws in the past decade's general approach of "integrating women in development." It has often implicitly been assumed that the development strategies being pursued are generally beneficial to the poor; thus, women's only problem is that they have been marginalized from the development mainstream. This approach has cast its shadow over much of the decade's debates, literature, research, and action. Even the evaluations of women-specific projects have focussed on their efficacy in terms of implementation, and rarely on their linkages to overall development strategies or processes. Nevertheless, it is worth pointing out that though marginal in terms of resources and scope, many of the projects of the Decade have provided women with skills, training, experience, and a sense of power that they would have otherwise found difficult to obtain.

Population Programmes and Reproductive Rights

The increase in relative inequality and in the number of people living in absolute poverty has often been attributed somewhat simplistically to rapid rates of population growth. This ignores the fact that in many instances growing poverty is linked to reduced access to arable land, lack of grazing rights for cattle, privatization of previously common waste or forest lands, and difficulties in obtaining water or other resources due to the pressures and incentives for profitable commercial cultivation. The dispute about the roots of surplus population can be traced back at least to Malthus and Marx. While Malthus held that human populations have a natural propensity to outstrip resource availability, Marx believed that the roots of surplus population are social. In particular, he argued that in capitalist society population is not excessive relative to natural resources but to employment, since the system has inherent tendencies to recreate job scarcity and unemployment. Thus it is only those with means of survival other than wage labour who appear constantly to be in surplus.[77]

The early programmes of population control in the Third World tended simply to assume that poverty could be reduced by limiting societal fertility, which could be effected through wide dissemination of contraceptive technology and knowledge. The recognition that many of the early programmes simply did not work generated a spurt of research into the factors underlying fertility behaviour. Some of the literature held that rural poverty, the economic roles of children, and concern of old-age security, as well as patterns of property inheritance were major causes of high fertility rates.[78] A major turning point in terms of policy was reached at the Bucharest population conference in 1974. The need to move away from narrow, technology-oriented family planning programmes to strategies that located these programmes within a broader perspective of improving health and education was recognized. It has also come to be argued that poverty and female illiteracy are prime breeders of high fertility, although the evidence on this score is somewhat ambiguous.[79]

In its World Development Report of 1984, the World Bank identifies the following as key incentives to fertility decline: reducing infant and child mortality, educating parents (especially women), and raising rural incomes, women's employment, and legal and social status. While this recognition of the links between women's autonomy over their lives and fertility control is to be lauded, multilateral agencies and national governments continue to treat women in an instrumental manner with respect to population programmes. For example, there is little understanding among policy makers of the mixed responses to family planning programmes by Third World women themselves. While there can be little doubt of the considerable unmet need for birth control among women, the methods actually available are all highly unsatisfactory. Many international pharmaceutical companies treat Third World women as guinea pigs for new methods; chemicals such as Depo Provera (which is banned in most advanced industrial countries as dangerous to health) are widely dispensed to Third World women, often with the knowledge and participation of international agencies.

The negative aspects of available contraceptive technology are insufficiently researched by the agencies or by national governments, which often find it convenient to accept the findings of the private firms producing the products. Nor are the specific problems experienced by poor women given much credence or importance. More and more evidence being unearthed by concerned women activists and researchers shows that, under Third World conditions of sanitation, health care, and female nutrition, many of the contraceptive methods being promoted can have serious side effects and even result in infertility. For example, the problem with intrauterine devices is not just that they alter bleeding patterns and therefore "may be culturally unacceptable or restrict the activities of users".[80] Often IUDs are inserted in rural women without proper sanitation or after-care. The heavier bleeding takes a severe toll on an already undernourished woman suffering from iron deficiency anemia. The need for an early return to hard labour after insertion, to which most rural women are accustomed, worsens the situation. Female sterilization especially when done in temporary sterilization camps, has similar hazardous effects.[81]

In the context of the development of more invasive techniques (e.g. IUDs and hormonal implants), the trend toward making birth control more "woman centred" can have negative implications for women.[82] It lets men off the hook in terms of their responsibilities for fertility control and places the burden increasingly on women. If women's own ambivalence toward contraceptive technology is to be removed (and this is crucial to any programme short of forced sterilization), the technologies themselves must become better adapted to the social and health environments in which they are used.[83] International agencies and national health ministries also need to establish higher standards for the testing and delivery of contraceptive techniques.

Governments do not view women instrumentally only when it comes to limiting fertility. In some situations they are interested in promoting births among certain sections of the population while limiting them in others. Government programmes in Singapore, which attempt to increase the fertility of educated women while reducing that of others, display both naiveté and class biases. Similarly, in some European countries there is an expressed concern over the relative differentials in the fertility of indigenous women vis-à-vis immigrants from their former colonies.

Control over reproduction is a basic need and a basic right for all women. Linked as it is to women's health and social status, as well as the powerful social structures of religion, state control and administrative inertia, and private profit, it is from the perspective of poor women that this right can best be understood and affirmed. Women know that child bearing is a social, not a purely personal, phenomenon; nor do we deny that world population trends are likely to exert considerable pressure on resources and institutions by the end of this century. But our bodies have become a pawn in the struggles among states, religions, male heads of households, and private corporations. Programmes that do not take the interests of women into account are unlikely to succeed. More important, the requirements of a genuine, people-oriented development necessitate the acknowledgement of this fundamental need and right.

In this regard, as on the issues of resources, income, and work, the problems of poor Third World women are inextricably caught up in the overall development process, and therefore must be addressed at that level and in a manner that acknowledges and builds on women's responsibilties in producing goods and "reproducing" human beings. Only in this way will societies be able to tackle the full-blown crisis of reproduction (in its broader sense) that now afflicts the poor, both women and men. It is to the lineaments of that crisis, and to the possibility of discovering new visions and strategies that will strengthen poor people, that we turn in the next chapters.

// 2 //

Systemic Crises, Reproduction Failures, and Women's Potential

At the outset let us spell out the distinction between the two types of crisis that afflict us today. The word "crisis" has been so over-used that it is important to clarify what we mean by it. When a structure or system reaches a stage when it must either undergo major changes or break down, it is in a state of crisis. Temporary solutions may mitigate some of its *effects*, but so long as its main structural causes remain untouched, the crisis persists, demanding resolution, and things cannot go back to "business as usual."

In this sense we argue that a crisis now affects both the world economic system and the structures through which the majority of the world's populations reproduce themselves. By reproduction we mean the process by which human beings meet their basic needs and survive from one day to the next. Since most people are part of a larger economic system – regional, national, or international – their own reproduction is not independent of the healthy functioning of the larger system.[84] But the two are by no means congruent. The economic system may show vigour and dynamism while people's basic needs remain unmet, or even worsen.[85] On the other hand, the basic needs of the poor may be met although the growth rate and per capita income remain low.[86] The reproduction of human beings depends to a considerable extent on state policies toward the agrarian sector, toward employment, and toward direct expenditures on basic needs fulfillment and poverty elimination. In the absence of explicit policies to meet the basic needs of the poor, economic growth will improve the conditions of human re-production *only* if it increases the employment and real incomes of the population at large. For example, export cropping in a previ-ously self-provisioning area may reduce people's access to land/ other resources without increasing employment, or even if it in-creases employment, it may not do so in a way that makes up for the loss of land access. The state may step in under such circumstances to make up the deficit through job creation or subsidised food. But once the onus falls on the state, reproduction of the poor becomes contingent on the exigencies of state expenditures.[87] A crisis in state spending under economic and/or political pressures can create a crisis of basic reproduction. This has been the recent experience of a number of countries that have cut subsidies on food and other mass consumption items under IMF pressure as a precondition for obtaining balance of payments loans.[88]

In this chapter we establish the links between the current systemic crises and the past history of development policies and strategies, the implications of the systemic crises for the reproduction of the poor, and the importance of recognizing women's potential for mitigating some of these effects through their position as the key human elements in basic reproduction.

The Food-Fuel-Water Crises[89]

It is our contention that although significant changes have occurred in the policy climate – in part because of the devastating impact of the Ethiopian famine – certain crucial aspects of the long-term problems of food availability not only in sub-Saharan Africa but in other parts of the Third World, are not yet sufficiently acknowledged at the highest policy levels. The neglected aspects have to do with women's critical position in societies as food producers, providers, and managers. Neglecting women's work in this case is not only detrimental to women, it also makes it impossible to develop the integrated approaches to the interlinked problems of food-fuel-water that are increasingly being recognized as essential to the success of policy.

For reasons of brevity we do not elaborate here on the policy differences and debates among different international development agencies, aid and research institutions, and national governments over the course of the three United Nations Development Decades. Rather, we focus on broad trends in actual policy and their effects. We argue that there has been excessive emphasis on aggregate food production and the grain trade at the global/national level to the detriment of land and resource availability for regional and local food self-sufficiency. This emphasis has made it difficult to perceive clearly the underlying fragility of the ecological, institutional and social bases of food-fuel-water availability and access in the Third World. Concomitant with this policy framework was the near total neglect of local food producers during much of the 1960s, the links among the availability of food, rural energy sources, and water, and women as the human element in those links. Although this neglect appeared to lessen in the 1970s, policy shifts have not averted such crises as those in the Sahel and Ethiopia.

During the major part of the first and second U.N. Development Decades, there were two identifiable strands in food policy. One strand stressed that efficient use of global economic resources required an expansion of *global* agricultural production and trade based on comparative cost advantages in that production.[90] Given that some of the major countries of the North – the U.S., Canada, and Australia – were already large commercial grain producers, while many Third World countries have historically specialized in the production of export crops such as coffee, sugar, cocoa, tea, and fruit, the proponents of this approach argue that production and trade should logically continue along these lines. Thus, world grain production has continued to be dominated by the U.S., Canada, and Australia while Third World farmers were encouraged to expand production of export crops in line with their apparent (historically established) comparative cost advantage. Food aid drawn from surplus grain stocks of the North was supposed to supplement grain availability in the Third World in periods of drought, floods, or other serious disruptions in agricultural production.

The second policy approach shifted the emphasis from global to *national* food production. This took effect mainly in those Third World countries which were already significant producers of wheat, rice, and corn. A "green revolution" was heralded in the 1960s, based on the dissemination of packages of high-yield seeds, fertilizer, pesticides, and water. The new technology was developed through a globally linked network of research institutes. It received government backing in the form of credit, marketing, and price supports, and was expanded consistent with an approach of "building on the best." That is, attention was focussed on those regions and farmers within a country who were most capable of helping themselves as individual producers; this was seen as most likely to obtain the maximum return to governmental resources.

Both approaches almost single-mindedly emphasized expanding agricultural production and trade, and providing the incentives for so doing. The difference between the two strands was that one argued for expanding global food production and international trade, while the other stressed national food production and internal trade within a country. This difference has been significant for questions of national self-reliance in food. Those Third World countries which took the former route (many countries in Africa and Latin America) and expanded exports or non-food production for the internal market have found themselves increasingly and uncomfortably dependent on world trade and aid. Since prices of agricultural commodities tend to be volatile in world markets, reliance on trade often means increased reliance on food aid when prices of a country's exports drop sharply. The irony here is that favourable climatic conditions leading to a large world supply of an export commodity and a resulting fall in its price can create the conditions for food aid by putting pressure on the balance of payments. Thus food aid may become necessary both under adverse and beneficial agro-climatic conditions.

Second, the structure of the international grain market, which is controlled by a few "merchants of grain," means that even the *purchase* of food grain in times of national scarcity may not be possible. The large grain traders have lobbied effectively against setting up a multilaterally controlled global food grain buffer stock, since this would reduce their ability to profit from the supply and price volatility of world grain markets.[91] Thus, for example, during the severe 1972–73 drought in India, the absence of a multilateral stockpile may have contributed to as many as a million deaths, since India could not afford to match the prices offered by China and the U.S.S.R. for U.S. grain.[92] Third, excessive reliance on food imports in a country that faces serious balance of payments deficits and an external debt burden makes national food availability vulnerable to these pressures as well.

Countries that have followed the "green revolution" route and expanded national grain production have been able over time to avoid some of these problems. For example, by the early 1980s Indian grain production and national buffer stock had become sizable enough that drought years could now be tided over more easily than before. However, even in such countries, the adverse distributional effects of a policy of "building on the best" have meant that increases in total national food production have not always been translated into food *access* among poorer regions, occupational classes, or income groups. Thus, while the national capacity for avoiding famines has undoubtedly improved in India, long term undernutrition among the poor has not been eradicated. Nor can it be claimed that the removal of undernutrition is only a matter of time, since overall production has increased. An important distributional effect of the "green revolution" policy is the relative and absolute channeling of resources away from the crops (e.g., millets, pulses) that are the staple diet of poorer regions and groups. Stagnant production means stagnant real income, which in turn means that structural undernutrition may worsen even as the national capacity to deal with the effects of drought improve.[93]

These distributional inequities have been especially harmful in Latin America and Asia. In many parts of Latin America the traditional co-existence of large estates and small tenancies has increasingly given way to capitalist and corporate farming with wage labour via dispossession of small farmers.[94] The result has been large scale population shifts to urban slums, rural impoverishment, and the growing dependence of the landless on seasonal migratory or contract labour on export farms. Land reform is therefore a major popular demand. In Asia the presence of large-scale unemployment and underemployment among the rural landless have made employment generation a major need, though here too land reform is essential.[95]

This leads to the wider question of food policies in the presence of large regional inequalities as well as inequalities in landholding. In Brazil, which claims to be the world's fourth largest grain producer, it is the poor who appear to have borne the main burden of the last six years of drought in the northeastern part of the country. The presence of extreme inequalities in landholding and politico-economic power in the region have meant that most drought relief measures and resources have been appropriated by the large landowners.[96]

The Sahel famine of 1968–73 brought some of these problems into sharp focus. Partly as a result there has been growing recognition in the policy-making community over the past decade that droughts are not purely "natural" disasters to which short term relief measures are an adequate response. A significant number of them appear, rather, to result from longer term structural factors thrown up by the regional patterns of development and land use. Resulting from this recognition, the Club du Sahel and the Permanent Interstate Committee for Drought Control in the Region (CILSS) agreed that food self-sufficiency should be the main goal of national and regional development.[97] Similarly, some research efforts supported by the U.N. and even bilateral aid agencies are now underway to explore the impact of cash cropping on subsistence food production. These efforts would do well to take account of the reasons for the continuing crisis in the Sahel.

Critical among those reasons is the lack of *integrated* policies toward farming, timber use, and water management. The crises of food, water, and rural energy are linked together through environmental and demographic processes, themselves the result of short-sighted policies and existing power structures. While drought is the single most important cause of food failure, drought is not caused exclusively by a shortage of rainfall. At least three types of drought can be identified: precipitation drought, runoff drought, and aquifer drought.[98] Even in years of normal or good rainfall, drought due to poor runoffs or low aquifer levels may have a devastating impact.

These two latter types of drought often result from deforestation and soil erosion caused by poorly planned and unbalanced tree cutting for industrial uses (pulp and paper mills, furniture factories, etc.), tree cutting for urban and rural energy or domestic energy needs under conditions of shortage, damming, and diversion of perennial rivers or streams for hydro-electric purposes, and overgrazing or unsound agricultural practices. Two major agroclimatic features characterizing large parts of the tropics exacerbate these problems: the thinness and poor quality of topsoils and the severity of seasonal rainstorms. The latter tend to wash away and compact even the existing soils in the absence of adequate vegetation and tree cover. Severe droughts now appear to have become endemic in sub-Saharan Africa. In 1984, according to the FAO, severe food shortages prevailed in Ethiopia, Sudan, the Sahel, and the southern African countries of Zimbabwe, Mozambique, Angola, Botswana, Lesotho, and Zambia.[99] The underlying processes are in operation outside Africa as well.[100]

Not all of the problems are attributable to excessive industrial use of forests. The privatization of previously waste and common lands reduces the availability of woody biomass (twigs, small branches, deadfall, and crop residue) that is the dominant form of domestic energy, especially among poor households in Africa. This leads to severe rural energy shortages, which are worsened by rapid rates of population increase.[101] In addition, the poor and landless also tend to lose access to forest produce as food and as sources of income.

A related effect of all these pressures on rural energy and water is growing soil erosion and declines in food production and productivity. The three crises – food, fuel, and water – are therefore interdependent and require integrated and longer term solutions. The need for such solutions is now beginning to receive systematic acknowledgment. For example, with funding from the Swedish International Development Authority (SIDA), the Swedish Red Cross and Earthscan (a London based international environment and development information service) have collaborated to produce the report by Wijkman and Timberlake cited earlier. Their main argument is that so-called "natural disasters" are to an increasing extent structurally caused by humans. While this is a depressing thought when one considers the scale of human misery involved, it also offers the hope that long-term policy solutions and options do exist and can be identified and implemented.[102]

The report sharply criticized from an insider's perspective the practices and motivations of agencies engaged in disaster relief. One of the main criticisms is that – like the proverbial bull in a china shop – relief agencies often disrupt existing social mechanisms for coping with disasters, foster external dependence rather than self-reliance and treat the poor (those usually affected most severely by disasters) as helpless victims. The report argues strongly, therefore, for the need to work out long term solutions in conjunction with local people, drawing on both their experience and stated needs, with policy and programme support from higher levels of decision-making.

If there is a fault to be found in this thoughtful and perceptive document, it is that it does not take the final and critical step implicit in its own argument. Namely, if food-water-fuel crises are interlinked, and if local people are to be the backbone of development efforts aimed at their resolution, then women (especially poor and landless) must be explicitly recognized as the key human elements in those linkages, and as active agents in any resolutions. What has been called a generalized reproduction crisis in the provision of "basic needs" has poor women at its centre, as the principal providers of those needs.

The importance of women to the solution of the generalized reproduction crisis is multi-dimensional. *First*, a large literature now shows that in many parts of the Third World women are important, often the main producers of food crops.[103] *Second*, even where women do not actually cultivate crops, they are almost universally the main food processors and cooks. *Third*, in addition to being food providers, women are usually also responsible for water and fuel collection, even though the labour of children is often quite important to the latter.[104] The less available are rural fuel and water, the more time women must spend in their collection. Evidence from national level sample surveys also now shows that poorer women perform these tasks in disproportionate numbers.[105] *Fourth*, the reproduction crisis is reflected in women having to make trade-offs among different basic needs in the use of such resources as their labour time, their cash income, or land over which they have some control. Where women have little earning power or effective control over cash income or land use (and this may be due to both traditional gender hierarchies and biased state policies toward land reform), their own labour time and that of their children (especially daughters) is the only resource over which they have any control whatsoever. Thus women's work hours, as the only mechanism for attempting to cope with the crisis, lengthen considerably. *Fifth*, the nutritional and health impact of these pressures operate through switches to less nutritious but less labour and fuel intensive foods, e.g., from yams to cassava, from millet to manioc, from whole grains to purchased processed foods.[106] This particularly affects the nutritional status of growing children. *Sixth*, women as managers of intra-household food distribution usually eat after men, and sometimes after children, thereby consuming smaller and less nutritious amounts. Also daughters are often discriminated against in favour of sons in food distribution.[107] In conjunction with increased work burdens, this leads to an absolute and a relative decline in women's nutritional and morbidity status.[108]

It is clear that women, as the main workers in basic needs provision, are central to an understanding of the linkages in the reproduction crisis. And it follows that women must be key potential actors in any resolution of the crisis. Indeed, with or without international or governmental recognition, women have already been organizing themselves. In India, for example, there is a spreading movement of women organizing against forest contractors to prevent deforestation.[109] Traditional kin and community based systems of mutual aid and self-help, e.g., "harambee" in Kenya, are vitalized for collective solutions to fuel and water problems. The existing women's groups tend to be local and participatory, as well as highly flexible in their ability to switch from one project to another as needed.[110]

A major barrier to the effective functioning of these groups is that the interests of poor men and women are not always identical, because of the existing sexual division of labour and resources. For example, men may be more interested in cash crops than in food crops if they control money income; they may be willing to sell forest rights to timber contractors; or they may be indifferent to labour-reducing technological improvements in cooking or fuel and water use. Some men may also fear the growth of women's power through collective organization and decision-making. The activation of women's organizations is key to the potential betterment of *all* the poor, and this is a critical argument in raising the consciousness of poor and landless men.

Governments and international agencies also continue to blithely ignore the mounting evidence that women, as the main providers of basic needs, are crucial to understanding and resolving the crisis of rural reproduction in the Third World. It is more than time to reverse this indifference. In a recent workshop on women's role in food self-sufficiency the working group on macroeconomic policies concluded that key regional requirements were: for Africa, the linking of food policies to women producers' access to land, credit, technology, and markets with greater overall emphasis on traditional grains and mixed cropping; for Asia, ensuring that food processing technologies do not continue to displace women, and that women be aided to set up co-operative rice mills, for example; for Latin America, that women be given equal status with men in land reforms and co-operative farming strategies.[111]

The Balance of Payments and Debt Crisis

Although insofar as Third World countries are concerned, a crisis exists in the form of unmanageable debt burdens and balance of payments deficits, these are but symptoms of a larger crisis in the post-war world financial and monetary system, as well as in the related mechanisms of international trade and capital flows. In the Bretton Woods system, despite the intentions of at least some of its founders,[112] the onus of adjustment to imbalances in international payments falls entirely on deficit countries. Given the structural weaknesses with which most Third World countries were saddled in the colonial era, their role has been one of perennial "adjuster." The U.N. Economic Commission for Latin America (ECLA) has extensively argued the need for inward-oriented, import-substitution strategies to reduce balance of payments pressures, and to give economic growth an internal momentum.[113] Simultaneously, ECLA favoured land reform as a mechanism for increasing agricultural productivity, reducing income inequality, and expanding the domestic market for industrial commodities. The mixed results of the land reforms undertaken during the 1950s, 1960s, and 1970s have been documented.[114] On the import-substitution side the mid-1960s saw the beginnings of a growing disillusionment and even reversal of earlier policies. It was argued that the "easy" phase of substitution in consumer goods would have to give way to a much "harder" phase of technology intensive capital goods production.

Most important, the import-substitution phase did not appear to have improved the balance of payments position of Latin American countries as had been its intention. Although the growing requirement of imports of capital goods and intermediates for domestic industrialization was blamed for this, insufficient attention was paid to another contributing factor, that by setting up protective barriers against imports, multinational corporations began to locate and expand industrial production in these countries. The extent to which the growth of industrial imports can be directly attributed to MNC production, the extent to which import bills were inflated by "transfer pricing,"[115] and the extent to which attempts to deepen domestic industry were weakened by multinational control and commercialization of technology are not fully known. Certainly all three did occur. But even apart from the imbalance on trade, the outflows due to profit repatriation and other such payments were considerable by the late 1960s. Thus, development strategies aimed at controlling trade while allowing relatively free capital movements could neither control trade nor improve the balance of payments.

By the late 1960s and 1970s export promotion was again becoming a dominant priority. After 1973 the recycling of petrodollars by commercial banks through lending to Third World countries is well known. While banks were eager to find profitable outlets for these funds, the loans were usually allocated according to priorities negotiated between governments, private lenders, and private borrowers (whose borrowing was sometimes guaranteed by governments). Rarely was there any accountability to the needs or interests of the people. Thus, as with other development policy making, neither the investment priorities nor the mechanisms were democratically determined. The loans were often spent for militarization, for infrastructure projects with long gestation lags, and in some instances for social services. There was also some leakage of the funds into foreign bank accounts.

With the slowing down of the world economy and world trade, the adjustment pressures on Latin American countries faced with large debt burdens became severe.[116] The rapid growth of the debt burden and the inability to repay are due in part to the current worldwide recession and the resultant decline in exports from Third World countries, a problem worsened by protectionism in industrial countries. But the ballooning of the debt is also due to the operation of variable international interest rates, which are affected by the U.S. policy of managing its own domestic and balance of trade deficits through high interest rates and capital inflows. The consequent instability in the international monetary and financial system not only makes it difficult to service the debts in the short run, but makes long-term planning well nigh impossible. It is in this context that the structural adjustment packages being negotiated by the IMF and the World Bank, operating in tandem, must be understood.

First of all, the structural adjustment packages are unlikely to lead to the required increase in exports in the face of growing protectionism in the advanced countries. Second, if the export promotion programmes do succeed, especially in agriculture, they are likely to reduce domestic food availability to the poor. Third, this will have a detrimental impact on human survival because of the cutbacks in consumer goods imports, in domestic subsidies for items like food and fuel, and in expenditures on health and education. Indeed, the international agencies and the business community are well aware that the "hard" phase of debt management lies ahead, and that there will be considerable civil and political turmoil occasioned by their structural adjustments programmes.

Furthermore, although there is considerable pressure on Third World countries to "structurally adjust," there is precious little openness in the multilateral agencies or the governments of the advanced countries to structural adjustment of the system as a whole.[117] And unless adjustment burdens are shared between surplus and deficit countries,[118] and unless the most powerful countries stop living beyond their means, the crisis of the system will not be resolved.

As already mentioned, the roots of the Third World's balance of payments crises go back to *before* 1973 and debt expansion. The structural roots lie in the openness to private capital flows and the large outflows resulting therefrom.[119] Balance of payments weakness was therefore built into the production and trading system during the import-substitution phase and thereafter.[120] The debt overhang only heightened and precipitated the crisis.

It is equally clear that the basic needs of the majority of the population will now be a low governmental or multilateral priority. Although it is too soon for a systematic assessment of the effects of "structural adjustment" in the 1980s, informed guesses of the negative impact of cutbacks on nutrition, morbidity, mortality, child survival, sanitation, transport, and education are unlikely to be far off the mark.[121] Budgetary cutbacks will also be felt directly in public sector employment. If the experience of Chile after 1973 is an indicator, the further opening of the economy to free goods and capital movements, and increases in prices of imported inputs, will have a recessionary impact as small and medium-size firms go out of business.[122] Large-scale unemployment combined with reductions in social services led to rapid and severe impoverishment in Chile, while capital flight worsened the pressure on the balance of payments.

For women the "structural adjustment" programmes are likely to have a number of effects. The effect of stabilization programmes on women's employment will probably be mixed. Their employment in small and medium-size firms producing for the domestic market will tend to decline as these firms go out of business. On the other hand, if export-oriented industries expand under governmental stimulus, women's employment is likely to expand as well, since female workers tend to predominate in this sector. As is well known, although wages and working conditions may sometimes be somewhat better in the larger factories in free trade zones, the work is temporary with high turnover and severe discipline. Many women in export units work under sweatshop conditions with low pay and high job insecurity.[123]

In response to the debt crisis, international agencies have advised some countries to generate foreign exchange through further expansion of export agriculture. Women's employment in this sector has grown as a result. This employment, in agribusiness plantations or estates, bears strong similarities to Third World women's factory employment, in terms of working conditions and vulnerability to seasonal variation. An example is the commercial production of winter fruits and vegetables in Mexico.

Women's employment also tends to expand in services, commerce and in "putting-out" work. These are the so-called "informal" activities that grow together with increased work participation by women.[124] While poor women have always worked for wages, the pressures of the stabilization programmes on incomes and consumption force even more women (older and younger) into the search for jobs. Domestic employment also offers an outlet, although the impoverishment of the middle classes may reduce the demand for paid domestic servants. Thus, women's employment may increase as a consequence of the "structural adjustment" programmes, but it does so perforce and mainly under the negative conditions of the so-called "informal" sector.

The specific effects of measures such as import restrictions (adopted as part of structural adjustment packages) on the range of activities encompassed in this sector are difficult to predict. On the one hand, by blocking or reducing the influx of imported consumer goods and other manufactures, the demand for goods that can be produced locally may increase. Yet certain occupations that depend on imported raw materials or goods (e.g., types of vending or trading) would be harmed by import restrictions. The reduction in mass purchasing power as a result of the structural adjustment programmes translates into reduced demand for many goods, but there may also be a switch to cheaper goods produced in the "informal sector."

A second major impact of the IMF backed programmes on women is through cuts in social service expenditures. These cuts occur at the same time that demand for these services increases, resulting from growing unemployment and poverty. Restrictive fiscal policy implies that services such as education, health, social housing, subsidized food, and transport are reduced, eliminated, or become available only at much higher prices. The implications for women are threefold. *First*, since women are the main household members responsible for tasks such as cooking, cleaning, and health care, their work burden is likely to increase. For example, lower social expenditures on health combined with poorer nutrition will increase the demands on women to make up the difference through health care at home. The time women spend waiting in queues will increase as bureaucratic procedures tighten and service availability shrinks. More time may have to be spent at public water taps, health centres, etc. *Second*, since women are usually responsible for managing the household's basic needs, the pressures to reduce their own personal access to such services as health and education will grow. So also their nutritional status. *Third*, the school dropout rate of young girls is likely to increase as they are forced to substitute for older women in home tasks or as they are drawn into putting-out work or sweatshops in order to supplement the family's real income.[125]

As we mentioned earlier, the evidence for these effects is still being researched and collected.[126] However, there is already considerable evidence about the impact of governmental service cutbacks on women in advanced countries, particularly the U.S. While Europe differs in a number of respects from the United States, most notably in current unemployment levels and stagnating internal demand, the relative insulation of the social welfare state, and labour and income security policies, there are a number of parallel trends. But we confine our analysis here to the U.S. because it provides the clearest illustration of the negative impact of governmental policies on women and the poor.

No matter how poverty is measured, the number of poor Americans grew by more than nine million in just four years, with the greatest concentration among minorities and low-income white women. This represents the largest increase since the Government began collecting poverty figures in 1960. Female-headed households comprise the bulk of recipients affected by government fiscal and monetary policies. Well over one-third of all female-headed households are below the poverty line, and more than half of all black and Hispanic households headed by women live in poverty.

Even before the Reagan Administration took office in 1980, poverty programmes contained serious gaps. While the popular view in the U.S. is that substantial benefit increases were provided over the previous 10 or 15 years to the poor as a whole, the reality is that major increases during this period were to the elderly and to a small number of white male-headed households. Benefits in major programmes plummeted because they were not adjusted for inflation, and eligibility requirements changed such that many in need of assistance were excluded. During this period, the purchasing power of poor female-headed households declined, and many lost access to subsidized services.

Today, programmes targetted to low-income individuals and families comprise less than one-tenth of the federal budget. Yet, under the Reagan presidency, these programmes have received the deepest cuts. Sizable reductions have been made in the public assistance programme for poor single parent (primarily female) families, programmes providing basic health care coverage for low-income families and the elderly, low-income housing, public service employment and job training, and unemployment insurance benefits. Contrary to the claims of this Administration, these cuts do not represent actual reductions in overall spending by the federal government, but rather a shift from spending in domestic to military sectors. Military spending has increased by over 40 percent from 1980 to 1985, larger than the total of all decreases in domestic spending since 1980.[127]

While the majority of recipients of public assistance programmes are white, these programmes serve minorities in large numbers. Thus, while about 12 percent of the overall U.S. population is black, over 40 percent receive public assistance in the form of income transfers, food stamps, medical coverage, etc. In the past four years, black families lost more than three times as much in benefit reductions as the average white family.[128] Hispanics have been affected by the budget policies in much the same way, and poverty has been rising more rapidly among Hispanics than any other group.

These budget cuts were accompanied by a major realignment of the tax system favouring high income tax payers and large corporations. The tax benefits that were supposed to accrue to low-income families were more than wiped out by inflation (which pushes families into higher income tax brackets) and by rising social security taxes. Until 1981, the U.S. Congress had cut taxes to offset some of the effects of inflation on the tax burdens of the poor, but ended this pattern in 1981. Low and moderate-income working families have always paid a larger share of income taxes, but this share now greatly exceeds that paid by large corporations. In the 1950s and 1960s, corporate income taxes contributed 25 percent of all federal tax revenues. By 1983, corporate taxes provided just 6 percent of such revenues.[129]

These policies were justified as a means to break the cycle of inflation and recession, and to produce a long-lasting surge of economic growth. However, many analysts believe that the key structural weaknesses of the U.S. economy which produced the recession will also prevent a sustained economic expansion. Any positive upturns in the economy must be seen in the light of the low-depths of the recession from which they began. Many economic indicators have not rebounded to their pre-1981 position. While capacity utilization rose initially, it is still well below its usual peak. Unemployment in 1982 was at its highest in 40 years, and although the current rate has dropped back to 1981 levels, the number of long-term unemployed remains high.[130] The U.S. trade deficit has reached massive proportions, due in part to the long-run decline in the competitiveness of U.S. manufacturing and to more recent factors such as the overvaluation of the dollar and high interest rates (products of the Administration's tight monetary policies). For the first time since the New Deal, the U.S. has become a debtor nation.

The economic growth that has occurred has been due primarily to the expansion of service industries. The long-term shift toward a service-sector economy has resulted in a greater relative share of low-wage jobs than has been the case in an economy dominated by a heavily-unionized manufacturing sector. Federal tax laws favouring the substitution of machines for workers have also reinforced technological changes that both upgraded and downgraded a vast array of middle level jobs, and resulted in what some have called "the disappearing middle." There is now an even greater polarization of low-wage and high-salary jobs and hence, wider inequalities in the income distribution of workers. The effect of this shift for women has been mixed. Their employment has increased because of the expansion in such services as retail trade and insurance, and because of the growth in non-union plants, sweatshops and industrial homework characterizing the reorganization of older manufacturing industries. However, women's jobs are on the whole low-wage, low-status, and dead-end. In addition, there is increasing documentation of the growing importance of "informal sector" activities for women in urban and rural areas.[131]

If the cutbacks and trends have been so inimical to women in an advanced country, they will be even worse for poor Third World women who begin from a much lower level of basic needs fulfillment. However, women, individually and collectively, have been discovering mechanisms for coping with these problems.[132] It should be remembered that women are neither responsible for the crisis in the world system, nor can they be expected to resolve it. Such a resolution requires concerted action through multilateral negotiations among countries. But the solutions to the systemic crises that are being put into place (viz., structural-adjustment programmes) are creating a major reproduction crisis, especially in the indebted Third World countries. Since women are responsible for the basic needs of households, they are affected both as producers and as consumers of the means to fulfill those needs. It is not our intention to glorify women's role in household labour or in the "informal sector." Particularly in the context of the debt crisis, the interests of poor women appear to lie in joining their voices to the struggle for a more structurally sound international and national economic order. This is of particular importance given that the supposed scarcity of resources has not prevented spiraling military expenditures in both the advanced countries and the Third World.

Militarization and Violence

According to a recent United Nations study,[133] since 1945 armed conflicts have taken up to 21 million lives. Most of these casualities have occurred in the Third World; and where a meaningful distinction could be made, three out of every five fatalities were civilians. Children, women, and the aged/infirm are dominant among civilian casualities, and among the refugees resulting from armed conflict.[134]

This frightening increase in global violence has a number of related aspects: (1) a growing potential for armed conflict between nations as a consequence of growing military expenditure; (2) further growth of an industrial structure geared to armaments production and trade; (3) a growing number of military controlled governments, most of which have as their main raison d'être the suppression of internal dissent, (this must be seen in the particular context of widespread popular resistance to IMF-backed programmes for "structural adjustment" through domestic austerity); and (4) the mushrooming of a culture of violence against women in which "macho-ness" and brutality are dominant; its flip-side is contempt for women expressed through reactionary notions of women's proper place in society.

Military expenditure[135] has become the Pandora's box of the twentieth century. Since the mid-1930s the volume of military activity has increased thirteenfold. According to a recent U.N. Department for Disarmament Affairs report,[136] the largest military powers constitute the main engine of the arms race, due to their virtual monopoly of the development of advanced military technology, their overwhelmingly large share of world military production and exports, and the global character of their political and military interests. Six main military spenders[137] account for three-quarters of the world arms trade, for virtually all military research and development, and for nearly all exports of weapons and military equipment. All significant developments in armaments originate in the developed countries, and spread to the developing with greater or lesser time lags; in recent years the time lags have diminished for many types of conventional weaponry. Of the six major spenders, the U.S. and the U.S.S.R. account for the largest share in the global total of military spending and the international arms trade.

Since 1960 the buildup of forces, the growth of military expenditures, and the investment in advanced military technology through arms imports proceeded at a faster pace in the Third World than in the industrialized countries. Two-thirds of the arms trade is now conducted between developed and developing countries,[138] and virtually every developing country has had armed forces trained by major powers. The thirteen OPEC countries alone accounted for over 40 percent of the arms imported by all developing countries between 1975 and 1980. These purchases, plus those by Taiwan and South Korea, included weapons as sophisticated as those in the NATO-Warsaw Pact armouries.[139] In the four years between 1978 (the year of the first U.N. Special Session on Disarmament) and 1982 (the year of the second), world military expenditures exceeded $1.6 trillion.[140] It is estimated that roughly one-fifth of total miltiary outlays go into the growing stockpiles of nuclear weapons.

There has been considerable debate in the industrialized countries about the economic effects of militarization, specifically on the inflation rate, employment, and productivity/growth.[141] According to studies by Sivard and others, military spending creates specific inflationary pressures peculiar to it, via cost plus-profit contracts, large-scale waste, and rapid product obsolescence. To ensure first claim on scarce materials, labour, management and scientific talent, military buyers operate under less price restraint than civilian buyers, especially in the U.S. Few economies can prevent this privileged demand from spilling over into other markets.[142]

In those Third World countries which rely on arms imports, the inflationary tendencies operate more indirectly by putting pressure on the balance of payments and hence on the exchange rate. Among the twenty developing countries with the largest foreign debts, arms imports between 1976–80 were equivalent to 20 percent of their debt increase during that period; in four of the twenty, the value of arms imports was equal to 40 percent or more of the rise in debt. At least six countries that had to renegotiate their debt after 1981 had spent $1 billion each for arms imports in the five preceding years.[143] A recent Rand Corporation study[144] found that arms transfers have played a signficant role in the growth of Third World debt. During the 1970's, developing countries increased their military spending three times faster than industrialized countries. By 1980 Third World countries accounted for over two-thirds of the world's armed forces, and imported $20 billion worth of arms. Despite per capita incomes still averaging below $670 in 1979, the non-OPEC developing countries spent $64 billion on foreign arms between 1970 and 1979. The value of their arms imports was equivalent to half of all foreign economic aid received.[145] Arms expenditures have contributed considerably to balance of payments crises, pressures for devaluation, and the consequent upward pressure on prices of imported inputs, and hence on domestic prices generally.

In the advanced countries it has also been argued that arms spending carries high opportunity costs in terms of civilian jobs lost; dollar for dollar, more employment is created through public endeavours such as construction, transport, health, and education.[146] The latter also create more transferable job skills in the labour force. At a time when 10 percent of the labour force in the Western European countries and over 7 percent in the U.S. is unemployed, a major reevaluation of priorities appears necessary. In Third World countries that import arms, these expenditures have negligible employment potential, at a time when rough estimates put the proportion of the labour force that is unemployed or underemployed at approximately 50 percent.[147] Correlations have also been drawn between high military spending and slow productivity growth, but these conclusions are more questionable.[148]

As a result of military procurement in the arms-producing countries, the multinational arms industry is one of the most prosperous and powerful in the world. In 1982 alone, aggressive government promotion in foreign markets helped the arms business realize an estimated $150 billion in annual sales. This ranks in size just below the annual incomes of the world's fourteen largest economies.[149] An increasing portion of military production consists of weapons for export, to recover at least a share of the soaring costs of research, development, testing, and evaluation. This equipment – increasingly weapons with greater technological sophistication – carries several risks. The more sophisticated the weapon, the less proven and reliable are its capabilities. The equipment is more expensive to develop and test, and is subject to production uncertainties that may drive long term funding upward in unexpected and uncontrollable ways. Finally, when the weapons do come into use, they generate large continuing operation and maintenance costs. When a Third World country with a low level of scientific infrastructure or technical power acquires such weapons, not only does it divert resources that could go to domestic investment, it also remains dependent for maintenance and operation.

The diversion of resources to military uses applies to vital minerals and land utilization. The arms race is depleting vital mineral reserves in developing countries, which will either be deprived of their future civilian use or will find them much more expensive. Most developed countries are completely dependent on a small number of developing countries for the minerals essential to sustain or accelerate arms production. The degree of dependence among countries varies to the extent that their national reserves and technology might allow substitution, recycling or stockpiling. But the demand side of mineral exports and the supply side of arms imports are closely linked. In several cases the recipients of military hardware among the developing countries also happen to be the suppliers of important strategic minerals to the developed countries. In addition, the increasing military requirements for land are not without consequence. As countries increase their manufacture of modern weaponry and the size of their armed forces, the amount of land diverted for this purpose will grow. To the extent that it destroys croplands, grazing lands, forests, and ground transportation networks, the burdens on the poor in these countries become even greater.

The extent of resource diversion from more productive uses cannot be emphasized too strongly. For example, in the 1970s Peru spent about 20 percent of its government budget (i.e., 4 percent of its GNP), equivalent to $160 million a year, on defense. While 60 percent of this went to military salaries, etc., 40 percent went to import arms.[150] According to Sivard's estimates, in 1980 Third World countries together spent $117 billion on the military, $105 billion on education, and $41 billion on health. In the same year their public expenditures *per capita* were: military, $34 billion; education, $31 billion; health, $12 billion – while only 44 percent of the population had access to safe water. This diversion of resources toward destructive rather than productive ends occurs at the national and the international levels.

In 1982, developed countries spent 17 times more on military expenditures than on foreign economic aid. In other words, at the start of the Third Development Decade they were devoting 4.5 percent of their GNP to the military and 0.3 percent to foreign assistance.[151] By the 1980s, with growing bilateralism and threatened cuts in contributions to the International Development Association (the soft-loan window of the World Bank that lends on easier terms to the poorest countries), the share of aid for the least-developed countries had decreased signficantly.[152]

A study by Leontief and Duchin[153] employs an input-output model to assess the effects of different levels of global military spending to the year 2000. High levels of military spending lead to lower total output and personal consumption in most regions of the world. A cut in military spending in advanced countries, with increased aid to the poorest countries, would not reduce the gap between rich and poor countries unless accompanied by structural economic and social change; but it would improve the standard of living of the latter. While we are somewhat wary of this argument given the kind of "development" that aid has tended to foster thus far, there does exist a considerable *potential* for a productive diversion of current military expenditures. Indeed, there is an inherent irrationality in a situation where nuclear missiles can go from Western Europe to Moscow in 6 minutes while the average rural woman in Africa must walk several hours a day to fetch water for her family.

In a way, the rapid rise in military spending during the last two decades is not surprising given the large number of Third World countries that have come under military rule during the same period. While it is understandable that countries which had to go through wars of national liberation in order to dislodge colonial regimes or neocolonial dictators (e.g., Nicaragua, Angola, Mozambique, Vietnam) might at the outset need time to consolidate control before calling elections, the majority of Third World juntas have not come to power on the backs of popular struggles.[154] Indeed, many military juntas have taken power through military coups that repressed mass movements and the aspirations of the poor for a better life (e.g., Chile in 1973). The massive military expenditures of these countries furnish the trappings of power to political leaders, such as jet aircraft, honour guards, and a budget that absorbs hidden luxuries. Actions in the name of "national defense" have unlimited perimeters; the ideology provides the rationale for secrecy and human rights abuses.

In fact, there is considerable reason to believe that the growth in Third World military expenditures contains a signficant component intended for domestic repression and violence, rather than for "national defense." The growth in human rights violations, torture, and training schools devoted to the subjugation of civilian populations through physical and psychological violence has been more than amply documented.[155] What is insufficiently recognized is the link between domestic unrest, and the inequality, poverty, and rampant exploitation bred by development processes and strategies directed against the poor. No contemporary example is more striking than the political and economic crisis in Central America. It is widely recognised that acute poverty and sharp inequalities have fueled the guerrilla movements in the region. Few realise, however, that the poverty and inequality are themselves the result of a rapid expansion of export crops and cattle ranching, and the consequent alienation of large sections of the peasant population from the land.[156] This process has accelerated in the last two decades.

The unrest of dispossessed peasant or tribal populations continues to simmer in various parts of the Third World. An added twist arises if they are ethnic minorities or indigenous populations, such as the Maya in Guatemala. On top of this is the urban unrest occasioned by stabilization and structural-adjustment programmes. There appears, therefore, to be a vicious cycle. Development strategies biased against the poor create the conditions that generate popular opposition, which in turn breeds violence and repression from those in power. The military and paramilitary forces[157] step in at this stage, and in the process increase their share of the domestic budget and external aid. This further squeezes social expenditures and increases discontent. Powerful external forces, such as multinationals, are often involved in supporting domestic repression.[158]

Militarization affects at least one part of the Third World in a more direct and dangerous manner. For over forty years a numbe of South Pacific countries have played a pivotal role in U.S. global military strategy. The continued colonial status of many of these territories has facilitated their use and abuse as a testing ground for nuclear missiles by Western powers. Entire islands have been contaminated and rendered unfit for habitation, populations have been dislocated, and the incidence of cancer, birth defects, and other diseases has increased. Because of their strategic military interests in the region, Western powers have frustrated the independence struggles of these economically dependent islands by threatening to cut off all aid to them. The popular protests of the region are as much against colonial domination and exploitation that allow for the perpetuation of militarization as against nuclear testing itself.

The effects of militarization on women operate both directly and through changes in cultural norms. We have already discussed the effects of fiscal cutbacks on women. A fortiori these effects would hold when the cutbacks are occasioned by military expenditures. In addition, the use of force to resolve international and national conflicts has led to large numbers of refugees, many of whom are women, children, and the aged and infirm. Refugees are also created by the destruction of crops and food supplies. Women are not spared by military governments' repression of internal dissent. Sexual abuse and rape are standard methods of terrorizing female prisoners, refugees, and the civilian populations in affected zones. Militaristic governments often endorse a "macho" ideology that defines women's place as the home, and breed through the modern mass media, the notion of women as weak, corrupting, and corruptible. At the same time, violence against women is increasingly depicted in film, video, T.V., and magazines.

Though militarism in some ways represents the ultimate depths of class biased and male dominated cultures, it also calls forth the most courageous and tenacious resistance from women. From small groups of mothers protesting the "disappeared" in Argentina, El Salvador, Guatemala, and Chile in the face of overwhelming odds, to the women protesting the kidnapping of youths by the armed forces in northeastern India, to the women's peace movement in Europe, and women who are engaged in the "parliament of the streets" resistance movement in the Philippines, women's struggles against organized military violence have been growing. It must be remembered, however, that for poor Third World women, peace and the struggle against violence cannot be divorced from the struggle for basic needs, economic justice, national liberation and a development oriented toward these goals. *Peace cannot be separated from development just as equality cannot, because the conditions that breed violence, war, and inequality are themselves often the results of development strategies harmful or irrelevant to the poor and to women.*

A Crisis of Culture

Growing worldwide militarization is being matched by the unleashing of powerful social forces – national chauvinism, racism and sexism – that subdue the most oppressed sections of society and dissipate their ability to resist the policies being pursued. For women the dimensions of this crisis include growing violence within the home, attacks on their civil status, physical mobility and work outside the home, and attacks on their control over reproduction. Simultaneously there has been rapid growth in the dehumanization and sexual objectification of women in the media, as well as sex tourism and prostitution abetted by governments concerned with generating foreign exchange earnings.

These conflicting pressures are enmeshed in the growth of other forces of reaction with strong manifestations in the First World, in some cases perhaps even more virulently than in the Third. Thus it was in the U.S.A. and U.K. that the invasions of Grenada and the Malvinas served to whip up mass feelings of "macho" manhood and national chauvinism. In Europe racism against Third World workers has become rampant with the rise of unemployment and the economic slowdown.[159] In the U.S.A. the New Right political movement coalesced with the combined purposes of defeating the Equal Rights Amendment, eliminating women's control over fertility, and increasing military expenditures and foreign intervention and domination.

Third World counterparts to this attempt to return women to their "proper" subordinate position in the patriarchal family are many. Traditional religion is often used for this purpose throughout the world. There has been a sharp upsurge of fundamentalism in most major religions. In the U.S., fundamentalist Christian churches provide finance, personnel, and ideas to the extreme right wing's attacks on women. Popular fears over the breakdown of traditional family structures and culture have been played on, often in a carefully orchestrated manner. It must be remembered that the religious hierarchy often finds this a useful way to regain its slipping authority and control over people's lives. In Iran, an additional twist is the use of anti-imperialist struggles and slogans in which women's role as mother and housewife is once more glorified.

The state is often directly involved in these efforts to subjugate women and suppress dissent. The Reagan administration openly supports the activities of the right-wing fundamentalists. In Guatemala, former president General Rios-Montt (who was a member of an American-based Christian fundamentalist church) launched a counter-insurgency drive which resulted in the large-scale massacres and dislocations of the highland Indian populations. In Pakistan, Zia ul Haq attempts to please right-wing fundamentalist Muslims by sharply restricting women's legal and civil status. In Iran, after the overthrow of the Shah, the government has become a theocracy wedded to the subordination of women.

In each case, the irony is that the attempt to drive women back to their "proper" roles is sharply at odds with the reality that many women *have* to seek employment in order to feed their children and themselves.[160] The creation of an ideological climate against women working outside the home makes it easier for the government to cut back child care or health services, and for employers to justify paying even lower wages to women or to ignore statutory benefits such as maternity pay. There is also a strong element of "blaming the victim." Just as North African, West Indian, or South Asian workers are blamed for unemployment in Britain and France, and undocumented aliens in the U.S., women have also been held responsible for unemployment.[161] They are also blamed for not taking proper care of children, and for being responsible for cultural decadence, Western influences, etc.[162]

It is important for us to understand the contradictory impulses behind these phenomena. Historically, in unsettled economic and political times attacks on women often go hand in hand with reactionary tendencies and impulses. This was the case, for instance, in Nazi Germany, a situation now extensively documented.[163] In part it reflects male fears and anger over unemployment and loss of prestige in and out of the home.[164] It is also a reflection of the class differences among women themselves that act as barriers to understanding between women who work predominantly in the home (whether on family farms or enterprises or as housewives) and those who work outside the home. The needs of these two sets of women (and of sub-groups within them) are often different not only in terms of work, but also in terms of services such as child care, as well as physical mobility and civil status. Even when women's incomes are roughly equal, significant differences in the issues affecting their lives can be used to pit one group of women against another.

This is not the first time that women have been made pawns in the struggle between the forces of "tradition" and so-called "modernity." A top-down attempt by the state to improve women's civil status as a wedge against "traditional" power blocs in society often creates simmering tensions. If the "traditionalists" gain control over the state, women's rights become one of the first targets of attack. Iran during and after the Shah offers a prime example of this tendency.[165]

Traditions have always been a double-edged sword for women. Subordinate economic and social status, and restrictions on women's activity and mobility are embedded in most traditional cultures, as our research over the last fifteen years has shown. The call to cultural purity is often a thinly veiled attempt to continue women's subjugation in a rapidly changing society. But traditions and culture also divide women themselves, since traditions and practices often vary across classes in the same society.

The implications of the above for women are fourfold. *First*, the richness of traditional cultural forms (music, theatre, dance, etc.) have to be harnessed for the struggle to raise the consciousness of both women and men.[166] Third World feminists will not then be seen to be at loggerheads with the national and cultural stream. *Second*, the problems of *poor* women have to be given a central position, since the reality of their daily lives so often belies the fundamentalists' myth. *Third*, men's equal responsibility for upholding cultural traditions must be vociferously articulated. Whether in matters of dress, food and drinking habits, or as consumers of pornography, men are usually further removed than women from traditions and more responsible for cultural decline

Yet it is women typically who are blamed! *Fourth*, counter to the growth of right-wing fundamentalism is the growth of progressive actions and beliefs within the churches as expressed, for example, in the theology of liberation, which links the struggle for a more just economic, political and social order to the spiritual salvation of human beings. While these forces are often in women's interests, they are not without contradictions, particularly because of the opposition of the leadership in the Catholic Church to contraception. Nevertheless, there is considerable support for contraception among lay Catholics and the lower orders of the Church hierarchy. Alliances therefore could be made on specific issues and at the local levels, but these too vary across regions.

It is in the area of consciousness-raising and mass education that the Decade's projects have been most lacking, although scattered initiatives by women's organizations provide sparkling counterexamples. Mass education must be supported to counter the rapid spread of violent pornography in the modern media,[167] and to change the traditional perceptions of masculine and feminine. This can be accomplished through institutional education and mass movements. Support from agencies and governments can play a useful role in many countries, though not perhaps in all.[168]

Raising the consciousness of government and agency officials and functionaries is an ongoing necessity as it largely determines their ability to recognize women's potential for developing methods to mitigate and perhaps even resolve the various crises outlined earlier. This is the alternative to the path of growing repression of basic needs and human rights on which so many countries are embarked. Whether in terms of food production and distribution, preservation of sources of fuel and water, regulating fertility, or generating collective forms providing services such as health, women's potential is significant. Further, from a global perspective, women have demonstrated their ability to withstand and organize against violence and militarism. Our hopes, not just for a better world but for its very survival, depend on the broadening and strengthening of these initiatives.

// 3 //

Alternative Visions, Strategies, and Methods

Much of what we have said so far has been drawn from women's experiences with development. While we have emphasized and drawn the links between macro policies and their less than benign effects on the poor, especially women, the picture is not entirely negative. Women drawing on their experiences have developed great capacities for internal resilience and resistance. Women have also had positive experiences of their own – of collective nonviolent resistance to nuclear weapons, military death squads, and forest contractors. Women have learned to shed traditional submissiveness and withstand family and community pressures, and have begun to work together to improve economic conditions for themselves and others. Women have organized to use traditional cultural forms to raise the consciousness of men and women about injustice and inequality.

The experience of working in grassroots organizations and women's groups over the last ten years has led us to several fundamental realizations. First, our consciousness and ethics now need to be crystallized into a clear *vision* of what we want society to be like, and what we want for women. This does not mean an attempt to impose a uniform ideology from the top. Rather, we feel that the debate around the real, hard issues of development, peace, and equality has only just begun, and we need to reflect together on what we have learned from the diverse richness of our experiences.

Second, we need the *strategies* that will get us from here to there, take us beyond the small and fragmented efforts of a decade in which women have begun to understand the enormity of the task we have set ourselves, and also the depths of our strength and potential. Thus, in this chapter we address ourselves first to women, but also to agencies and governments.

Third, we want to spell out the *methods* for actualizing our visions and strategies through the empowerment of individual women and their organizations. It has been a strong theme of the modern women's movement that objectives and methods, ends and means are closely bound together. Our own life experiences as women have shown us how easy it is to suppress and subjugate in the name of a "greater good" if this principle is forgotten. The mass movements for peace and justice have an ethical basis that can strengthen and empower us if it is clearly understood and affirmed. The women's movement too can have an ethic drawn from women's daily lives. At its deepest it is not an effort to play "catch up" with the competitive, aggressive "dog-eat-dog" spirit of the dominant system. It is, rather, an attempt to convert men and the system to the sense of responsibilty, nurturance, openness, and rejection of hierarchy that are part of our vision.

Visions

Our understanding of feminism structures our visions for society and for women. We recognize that there can be diverse meanings of feminism, each responsive to the needs and issues of women in different regions, societies, and times. This is because of our understanding that feminism is a *political* movement, and as such expresses the concerns of women from different regions and backgrounds. Like all political movements, it can be diverse in its issues, immediate goals, and methods adopted. But beneath this diversity, feminism has as its unshakeable core a commitment to breaking down the structures of gender subordination and a vision for women as full and equal participants with men at all levels of societal life.

There has been considerable confusion and misunderstanding among women around this question. The recognition of the existence of gender subordination and the need to break down its structures has often led to the wrong conclusion that it engenders monolithic and universal issues, strategies and methods, applicable to all women in all societies at all times. But a political movement that is potentially global in scope needs greater flexibility, openness, and sensitivity to issues and methods as defined by different groups of women for themselves. *Self-definition* is therefore a key ingredient to relevant political action.

A recognition of diversity in issues and methods allows women to work for change within existing structures or to work to transform those structures. It allows women to challenge and debate the connections between various immediate issues and the ultimate vision of gender equality in more fruitful ways than dogmatic assertions of the "true" meaning of feminism. It makes it possible to form alliances with other organizations, to assert the need for autonomy, or to work within existing organizations as appropriate. It enables women to link the struggle against gender subordination to those against national, racial, and class oppression where these issues are bound together, and depending on the politics and potential of other organizations.

In the light of this conception of feminism, the vision for society put forward here is a dual one. Since poor women are the central actors on our stage, both poverty and gender subordination must be transformed by our vision. Insofar as poverty is concerned, its structural roots lie in unequal access to resources, control over production, trade, finance, and money, and across nations, genders, regions, and classes. We are well aware that given the enormity of the present gulf between rich and poor, and the fact that it has tended to widen rather than to shrink, these structures are unlikely to change quickly. But we must have before us a vision of the kind of world we want.

We want a world where inequality based on class, gender, and race is absent from every country, and from the relationships among countries. We want a world where basic needs become basic rights and where poverty and all forms of violence are eliminated. Each person will have the opportunity to develop her or his full potential and creativity, and women's values of nurturance and solidarity will characterize human relationships. In such a world women's reproductive role will be redefined: child care will be shared by men, women, and society as a whole. We want a world where the massive resources now used in the production of the means of destruction will be diverted to areas where they will help to relieve oppression both inside and outside the home. This technological revolution will eliminate disease and hunger, and give women means for the safe control of their fertility. We want a world where all institutions are open to participatory democractic processes, where women share in determining priorities and making decisions.

Perhaps we have said nothing new; indeed, it has been said before. It is often stated, however, that the world lacks the resources to meet the needs of all the poor, and that poor countries must increase their productive potential before mass living standards can be improved. Both of these statements are, as we have argued, patently false. The massive and growing resource diversion toward militarization gives the lie to the first, while the cited examples of countries which have grown rapidly without improving mass living conditions, and others which have done the reverse, prove that there is no simple congruence between economic growth and basic needs.

What is lacking is not resources, but political will. But in a world and in countries riven with differences of economic interest and political power, we cannot expect political will for systemic change to emerge voluntarily among those in power. It must be fostered by mass movements that give central focus to the "basic rights" of the poor, and demand a reorientation of policies, programmes, and projects toward that end. The opening of political processes to accommodate greater expression of opinions and dissent, as well as participation by poor people in the decisions that affect their lives at the macro and the micro levels, is crucial. In this regard, it is heartening that, despite the severity of the economic crisis (and in some instances through resistance to government programmes directed against the poor and middle classes), countries in Latin America and elsewhere have experienced a process of democratization of political processes. The power and potential of the women's movement must be tapped in expanding and safeguarding these gains.

The transformation of the structures of subordination that have been so inimical to women is the other part of our vision of a new era. Changes in laws, civil codes, systems of property rights, control over our bodies, labour codes, and the social and legal institutions that underwrite male control and privilege are essential if women are to attain justice in society. The consequences of the prevalent injustices and inequities in terms of women's health, work burden, access to employment and income, and even mortality rates are well documented. Only by sharpening the links between equality, development, and peace, can we show that the "basic rights" of the poor and the transformation of the institutions that subordinate women are inextricably linked. They can be achieved together through the self-empowerment of women.

Strategies

What do our experiences suggest about strategies for change? As we have seen, women's income and employment generation projects have suffered by being scattered, small, and peripheral to the main thrust of planning processes, programmes or projects. Different agencies (international and national) have financed a plethora of small projects in various sectors with little coordination nor concern for sustained financial viability, capacity to grow and expand, or replicability. Despite these drawbacks, the very smallness of projects has enabled women to understand how to cope with local power structures, how to articulate demands, and how to use organizational strength to counter gender biases and rigidities inside the home.

In moving beyond this initial project experience, we need to situate our goals and actions within the context of the larger vision we outlined. Improving women's opportunities requires long-term systematic strategies aimed at challenging prevailing structures and building accountability of governments to people for their decisions. Short-term, ameliorative approaches to improve women's employment opportunities are ineffective unless they are combined with long-term strategies to reestablish people's – especially women's – control over the economic decisions that shape their lives. Women's voices must enter the definition of development and the making of policy choices.

These are strategies that must be debated, first of all, within the women's movement and among grassroots women's organizations. Such discussions can help to genuinely incorporate the experiences and concerns of poor women, to discern and identify regional and local variations, and to articulate a consolidated body of analysis and programmes to ourselves, as well as to national governments and international agencies. Any effective strategy must integrate economic, political, legal, and cultural aspects. For the sake of simplicity, however, we have divided our discussion between these different spheres.

The *economic* sphere should distinguish between the long and short-terms. In the *long run* we need strategies that will break down the structures of inequity between genders, classes and nations, which act as barriers to development processes responsive to the needs of people. Planned changes must reorient production processes in agriculture, industry, and services, so that meeting the needs of the poor becomes the principal focus of planning. In this context, recognition not just of poor women's work but of its *centrality* to such development processes is essential, as is the need to make poor women central to both planning and implementation.

Requisites for such a fundamental change in development orientation are national liberation from colonial and neocolonial domination, and national self-reliance, at least in basic requirements such as food and energy sources, health care and water provision, and education. This will in many instances involve a shift from export-led strategies in agriculture and industry, where such strategies have demonstrably been inimical to the basic needs of human survival. As we have argued, women's long-term interests are consistent with such a reorientation, even though women are the dominant workers in export industries and agriculture under present production structures.

Another important strategy needed to reorient development is a worldwide reduction in military expenditures and resource use. As we have shown, there are close links between growing military budgets and poverty in the industrial countries, on the one hand, and diversion of resources, depletion of minerals, suppression of dissent, armed conflict, and distortion of development priorities in the Third World, on the other. Of course, the interdependence between dictatorial regimes and external economic and geopolitical interests is close in most instances. But with growing liberalization of political processes, at least in some countries, there is considerable scope for building a popular climate against militarization. Women's organizations can play a crucial role in this.

On the international front, demilitarization strategies are linked to Third World priorities in another important way. The contribution of rising military expenditures to budget deficits, high interest rates in the U.S., and growing debt burdens in the Third World has already been noted. Therefore, a reduction in the U.S. military budget could potentially reduce the pressure on the balance of payments of debtor countries and hence the burdens imposed by structural adjustment on the poor and middle classes in these countries. As we noted, a very large share of these burdens falls on poor women, who lose incomes and access to services, and who have to make up for this loss through an increase in their own labour.

The control of multinationals is another long-term requirement. Large corporations have been instrumental in diverting resources from basic needs toward commercialization, exports, and militarization. The employment they create in the Third World tends to be small in volume and to consist of dead-end jobs. The technology they sell is often unsuited to the consumption needs of the majority, and to domestically available resources. The outflows of profits, interest, and royalities place considerable pressures on the balance of payments as well. Greater control over the activities of multinational corporations is therefore a critical ingredient for national self-reliance, which is in turn essential for equitable development.

In many countries the transformation of internal inequities is closely linked to the above strategies, since dominant internal classes and groups are often closely allied to external economic and political interests. In addition, needed changes in the rural areas must be predicated on genuine land reforms. The production organizations that emerge after such reforms will vary, depending on technology, cropping patterns, and the extent of landlessness that might persist even after reforms. We shall not elaborate on these here, beyond making the point that women must be given equal status during and after reforms, from the standpoint of equity and from the concerns of agricultural production and integrated fulfillment of such basic requirements as food, fuel, and water.

Proposing long-term strategies for major societal change may lead to cynicism because of the considerable chasm between the present situation and that projected in a vision. We face powerful interests internationally and nationally – dominant countries, internal ruling classes and groups, multinationals – opposed to our long-term vision and goals. *What are the strategic points of leverage* that women and other likeminded groups can identify and use in the struggle toward our vision of society? Since forces arrayed against us are by no means monolithic in their interests and aims, we must learn to use these differences strategically. A number of examples can be cited in this context.

On the question of food production in sub-Saharan Africa, for example, the Berg Report adopted by the World Bank, the Lagos Plan put forward by governments in the region, and the Reagan administration's proposals for agricultural production and aid are significantly at odds with one another.[169] While the Lagos Plan calls for greater self-reliance on the food front, the Berg Report emphasizes accelerated export production supplemented by food aid. The Reagan government has cut back on aid to all but five countries in the region which it views as strategic to U.S. interests. In this case, women's interests appear to be more compatible with the Lagos Plan, provided that the role of women in food production and marketing can be made more central. Similarly, on the question of debt, women's interests are connected to those national interests opposed to IMF adjustment programmes. Government expenditures for basic needs must become an inviolable budgetary item. Here again women can bring in additional perspectives based on their experiences of providing collectively-managed services for food provision, child care, health, etc.[170] We are not arguing that women should compensate for the loss of vital services by increasing their already heavy burdens (they are doing this individually in any case). But if provided with adequate funding, community control and participation by the poor can be a viable strategy toward raising people's consciousness through collective solutions to these problems. Vice versa, international agencies such as those in the United Nations system can also be used to exert greater pressure in the areas of basic needs, land reform, technology, and women's work and employment, as well as in national and international systems of data collection and planning.

Short run strategies must of necessity provide ways of responding to current crises, while building experience toward the longer vision. In the area of food production we advocate a shift toward policy packages that promote a more diversified agricultural base, leading to a safer long-term balance between export and food/subsistence crops. Women's expertise in food gathering and food production as well as in marketing and processing must be reinforced.

Even as they have been moving into cash crop production or off-farm activities, most rural women have retained a toehold in this sector, especially in Africa. In the current crisis, policies should mobilize women's experience and skills. Toward this end governments should ease restrictions and pressures on women petty traders and vendors, while increasing the availability of credit for the the self-employed women in this group.

An additional challenge is in the area of poor women's employment and income earning in agro-related activities, many of which have been severely eroded by mechanization. The major agricultural research institutes at the national and international levels should be turning their attention to technologies that will reduce drudgery without reducing employment. Women's organizations have been active in the area of appropriate technology in food processing and storage, water provision, and fuel, and these experiences can be utilized. We also need to redress the relative exclusion of women agricultural labourers from farm labour unions, which helps perpetuate lower wages and greater seasonality in their employment. Where food-for-work or employment guarantee schemes have been launched in rural areas, they have in some cases been used to provide cheap labour to large farmers at government expense. Such schemes should be strictly used to create employment in, for example, tree planting for local fuel, housing construction, water provision, and similar areas that will improve the basic needs of the local poor.

In the industrial sector, organization of workers in traditional industries (many of which tend to be female-dominated) is as necessary as in export industries and free trade zones. The problems of wage workers in this sector are somewhat different from those of self-employed women in the so-called "informal" sector. In petty trade and services women suffer particularly from police harassment, lack of credit, access to markets, and obstacles in obtaining licenses. Yet the informal sector is much larger than the "formal" in most countries, and more important, is more likely to be meeting the consumption requirements of the poor in urban and rural areas. Support for this sector and for women within it will pay off by helping them to meet the need for cheap basic goods and services in the current crisis.

It should be clear from our discussion that we do not expect the strategies suggested above to be implemented without sustained and systematic efforts by women's organizations and likeminded groups. Thus *political* mobilization, *legal* changes, *consciousness raising*, and *popular education* are core activities in the process we envisage. These have of course constituted a significant part of our efforts during the past years. Now we must draw together to consolidate and learn from our experiences and their diverse sucesses and failures. At the *global level*, a movement of women and the oppressed can mobilize support for the common goals of a more just and equitable international order, and for disarmament. A global network of likeminded women's organizations committed to these goals could exchange experiences and information, suggest action and provide support. We also need research programmes on those issues which can be best analyzed from a transnational or cross-cultural perspective for example, the links between gender subordination and global conservation measures, reform of the international monetary system and the IMF, and demilitarization.

In addition to global actions and programmes, involved non-governmental and women's organizations, politically active women's groups, and worker organizations can coordinate common action programmes at the *regional* and *sub-regional levels*. This is particularly important in supporting women in countries that are politically repressive or in which the state has attacked women's social and economic status. The initiation of projects on problems common to the region and the development of regional training and research insitutions can be useful steps in this direction. Such activities have grown in number and significance toward the latter part of the Decade.

In building movements at the *national level*, it is essential for us to develop a methodology for political action and political support to women's issues as they emerge, both on general questions and in a particular context. For this, coalitions and alliances (possibly cutting across different women's organizations and political affiliations) can help us to build a broad-based local and national movement. This too is essential in countries with repressive political climates. In some countries where class-based organizations are severely restricted, women's organizations may have some flexibility for action; in others the reverse is true. A broad- based movement, including mixed organizations across gender and class, may

offer the most viable route for fundamental change in many situations. A resource base of women activists can work toward the dissemination and acceptance of a common programme or ideology by other political and socially conscious organizations. Organizations of women and poor men to implement specific programmes and to work as pressure groups have already demonstrated their potential. Mobilization around specific laws and civil codes may also be required to complement these strategies. Here women's organizations can draw on the support of other socially conscious groups, and in return, provide support in struggles around civil liberties, political repression, and abuse.

The level of awareness about women's subordination has to be raised through popular culture, the media, and formal and informal education. Unfortunately, such activity is all too often seen as secondary or unrelated to the activities of politically-oriented organizations. But if we are ever to progress beyond peripheral projects and schemes for women, we need much more attention to consciousness-raising. Governments must be pressured to give us a greater voice in radio, T.V., film, and other mass media, and to generate more funding for such programmes. The role of women's studies in this process is important. We already know that research into our history, networking among scholars, and curriculum development are vital aids to raising our own consciousness, as well as that of men. But women's studies in the Third World cannot stay in the academy. Because large segments of our people are still illiterate or unused to the printed word (and this is even more true for women than for men), we need to concentrate on techniques for popular and mass education. This is where the methods learned in the "pedagogy of the oppressed" can be useful, and where local organizations can again play a crucial role. We must also educate lower-level planners and functionaries as well as activists, and make inroads into formal education. All this is essential if feminism and women's liberation are to be understood as relevant to the progress of all sections of the poor and oppressed in society.

Empowering Ourselves Through Organizations:
Types and Methods

Because women's organizations are central to these strategies, a more thorough examination of methods for their empowerment is necessary. Not only must they strengthen their organizational capacity, but they must crystallize visions and perspectives that will move them beyond their present situation. The strategic role of these organizations and networks can be seen from two perspectives. Developing the political will for the major changes needed in most societies requires organizations that have the strength to push for those changes, and the mass potential of women's networks in this area is great. Second, the particular perspective of poor women gives centrality to the fulfillment of basic survival needs as *the* priority issue; they are therefore the most committed, militant, and energetic actors once avenues for action emerge.

What methods for the empowerment of individual women and organizations can catalyze strategies and build movements for social change consonant with our vision? It is important to draw on existing organizational strengths while working out ways to overcome weaknesses and conflicts. Although many organizations suffer from class or other biases, we feel it is worthwhile to assess whether such biases can be overcome, and if not, whether there are particular issues or programmes on which organizations of poor women can work with other groups.

Empowerment of organizations, individuals and movements has certain requisites. These include resources (finance, knowledge, technology), skills training, and leadership formation on the one side; and democractic processes, dialogue, participation in policy and decision making, and techniques for conflict resolution on the other. Flexibility of membership requirements can also be helpful, especially to poor working women whose time commitments and work burdens are already severe. Within organizations, open and democratic processes are essential in empowering women to withstand the social and family pressures that result from their participation. Thus the long-term viability of the organization, and the growing autonomy and control by poor women over their lives, are linked through the organization's own internal processes of shared responsibility and decision making.

Since different types of organizations have different histories, weaknesses, and potential, we try below to spell out some of these differences in order to engender further debate. Our classification does not pretend to be exhaustive. Nor is it done from the usual viewpoint of donor agencies that wish to know which groups are the most suited to receive funding. It is done rather from the desire to build and strengthen our own movements and networks, that is, from the perspective of empowerment.

First, there are the major, traditional, service oriented women's organizations that are of long standing in many countries.[171] While such organizations have sometimes been criticized for having a "welfarist" approach, they have performed valuable functions in the areas of women's education, health, and related services. In the Third World context, such organizations sometimes arose within a context of generalized social reform movements or nationalist struggles. At the time they often represented the only major avenue for raising issues concerning women. We need to learn more about their histories in the face of struggle, and how they were able to grow. Such organizations usually have significant resources and access to policy makers, formal structures of decision-making and power, membership drawn from different sectors of society, and systematic methods for transferring skills and building leadership.

They tend to have three major weaknesses. They often suffer from class biases in their membership and programmes so that their major efforts are directed at middle and upper class women, while poor women are treated in hierarchical and patronizing ways. Their internal decision-making processes are usually top-down and allow little scope for participatory processes that empower all women, not a chosen few. And they often lack a clear perspective or even understanding of gender subordination or its links to other forms of social and economic oppression. Despite these flaws, we can learn a great deal from the ability of these organizations to raise women's issues in the public arena and marshal large-scale support for their agendas, often under adverse circumstances. Consciousness-raising in these organizations, especially those which direct their activities to poor women, can therefore have a worthwhile payoff.

A *second* major type of organization is that affiliated to a political party. The degree of importance of such organizations, their resource base, and their autonomy in raising issues for either debate or action varies considerably from country to country. Such organizations can raise issues related to organizing women workers within the context of parties that may already have considerable experience organizing peasants or male workers. Their problem is that they often find it difficult to address gender issues directly, even in this relatively familiar context, for fear of being labeled divisive to the struggles of workers or the poor. Thus, the question of autonomy is a key one for most such organizations. Some newer political parties, such as the Greens party in Germany, are more explicitly feminist both in orientation and internal structure.

A *third* type of potentially large organization is the worker-based organization.[172] This includes both formal trade unions of workers employed in the formal sector, and organizations of poor self-employed women, of which there are a growing number in the Third World. These two sub-types are themselves different in that the former contains examples of unions where women form the base, while most leadership positions are held by men; the latter groups have much better representation of poor women. The worker-based organization usually addresses issues of employment, incomes, working conditions, and availability of credit or marketing, and is more sensitive to such issues as childcare and the demands on women's time in the organization itself. Some of these organizations are explicitly aware of the character of women's subordination. But even those which do not overtly perceive themselves as feminist are conscious of the substantive issues of both gender and class as they affect poor women's lives. The experience and the potential of such organizations are encouraging, although their resource position may be weak, reflecting the poverty of their membership. Such organizations also tend to be very successful in empowering poor women in their own personal life situations.

A *fourth* type is the organizations that have mushroomed during the Decade as a result of the external flow of funds and interest. Many of these organizations have no previous organic history and little organizational or resource base independent of the project being implemented. Illustrations of this type of organization include the various handicraft or credit cooperatives set up by donor agencies. Some of these organizations match the structural weaknesses with a top-down approach, lack of understanding of the problems of poor women, and often class biases as well. Such organizations are among the weakest of the different types of organizations considered here, though many of them have persisted through funding generated during the decade. Others, however, have been more succcessful in evolving participatory styles.

A *fifth* type of organization is the grassroots organization which may be related to a specific project.[173] While similar in some respects to worker organizations, this category of groups does not engage directly in workplace issues. However, the problems they address are often economic in nature. Such groups may also focus on media, health, literacy, or violence. They often direct their work to poor and working women, provide various types of technical assistance to other groups, and engage in advocacy, legal struggles, and political action. Some of these groups are explicitly feminist in their orientation. Their weaknesses include an inadequate resource base and the fact that, in many instances, they tend to have a more middle-class, urban membership and perspective. But if their work with and among poor women can be strengthened, these groups have considerable potential.

The *sixth* organizational type is the research organizations that have been growing rapidly in the last few years.[174] These include groups involved in participatory action (and policy) research, women's studies associations, and research networks. Such groups have considerable potential to influence public policy debates, evaluate the programmes of agencies and governments, inform and feed research into other types of women's organizations, and link research with action. These groups aim to eliminate the distinction between the researcher and the researched, so that research becomes a process of mutual education. They are also committed to using their findings to serve and empower the subjects of the research. Their flaw is that they sometimes exacerabate tensions between researchers and activists by using the results in individualistic ways without benefitting those researched. This, however, may sometimes be more a problem of the individual researchers than of the organizations to which they are linked, but the organizations themselves need to be aware of this problem. The challenge facing these groups is to develop structures and methods

of accountability to both action organizations and the subjects of
the research, perhaps through stronger policy linkages or direct
services.

In addition to these six types of organizations, a large number of
women's movements (encompassing individuals, organizations,
and coalitions) have sprung up during the decade.[175] These cover a
multitude of issues and purposes but share a concern and identification with women's causes. Their overall strength derives from
their flexibility and unity of purpose, while their weakness may
stem from the lack of clear organizational structures (this can also
be a source of strength in a repressive political situation). Such
movements have come together around basic needs such as fuel
and water, and in response to urban crises such as loss of services
or inflation. They also focus on such issues as peace, opposition to
violence against women, sex tourism and sexual exploitation, militarism and political represssion, racism, and fundamentalist religious forces opposed to women's rights. Many of these movements
are large, mass-based, non-violent in their methods, and extremely
courageous in the actions undertaken. The tenacity and commitment of women in the peace encampments and in opposition to
military dictatorships are well known. Such movements are dyna-
mized by the issues, mass support, and energy of the activities of
individuals, smaller groups, and coalitions that are involved in
them. Between the organizations and the movements stand networks and coalitions, some of which are permanent and others
more temporary. Their goals range from direct political action to
exchanges of research and information.[176]

The organizations described here have developed a range of methods for reaching marginalized women and have made significant
contributions during the Decade. However, in order to move forward, it is necessary for us to experiment with creative approaches
and to analyse the conflicts and issues that challenge our organizations. The first is that many (but not all) women's organizations
have been wary of viewing large public policy issues as within their
purview. Two distinct but related tendencies explain why groups
have functioned outside this domain: on the one hand, feminism
has concerned itself, among other things, with aspects of life that
are only partially susceptible to institutional regulation. This is
true not only in the domestic sphere but also (and this is particu-

larly relevant in the Third World) in such spheres as the "informal" sector or clandestine economy. On the other hand, the marginalization of women's groups from public policy may also be due to the hitherto fragmentary character of our own vision, and our inability to articulate the links between development and equality.

The *second* problem arises in our search for non-hierarchical and non-formal organizational structures in a world increasingly formalized and hierarchical. In this context, we have not developed enduring and effective channels for acquiring representation. Frequently, a given organization does not clearly know who is a member. While this may be a useful tactic in confounding repressive regimes, it has made it difficult for us to establish clearly delineated relationships with complex and bureaucratized decision-making bodies and to successfully pressure them to implement policies in our interest.

A *third* set of problems occurs from women avoiding clear assignment of responsibilities or delegation of authority for fear of mirroring existing hierarchies or established power structures. Two difficulties derive from this stance. One is external: no one is authorized to speak for the women's movement, so that in trying to define public policies our voices are weakened. Another is internal: our groups are unstable largely because of inadequate resources, but also because of the total commitment (and resultant quick burnout) required of each person. If responsibilities are never defined, everyone is expected to do everything.

Why is it that many women have found it difficult to delegate organizational authority? Perhaps because our experience as women has shown that division of responsibility can be used as an instrument of subordination. Our mistrust must stimulate us, however, to devise innovative ways of sharing responsibilities so that we do not reinforce existing relationships of domination. And we must develop structures which keep leaders accountable and responsive to the voices and needs of the membership at all levels of the organization.

A *fourth* difficulty arises when we try to build alliances. Women have had too long an experience of being used by governments, agencies, or organizations for purposes not in our interest or of our choosing. As a result we tend to look with suspicion upon any political force or body that is not of our own making. Even othe women's groups in the same country sometimes come under attack. Especially given our vision of orienting ourselves to the mainstream of development activities and economic processes, we need to learn to ally ourselves more closely and effectively with other grassroots organizations without jeopardizing our autonomy or theirs. A process of dialogue and working on joint programmes is the only way to begin to build mutual respect for the strengths and capacities of each, and trust in each other's intentions.

A final issue is our ability and willingness to share power within our own organizations. Related to this is the question of our styles of conflict management and resolution. Such conflicts appear to come from two main sources: the first is genuine differences in strategies, issues, and evaluations of the organization's potential or internal biases; the second is that those with the dynamism, energy and genuine concern to start organizations are often afraid that others less well-motivated and more prone to personal aggrandizement will seize control over organizations built up with great effort. These fears are well-founded in some instances; they are compounded by the inflow of funds from international agencies that makes the takeover of organizations and their resources more tempting.

Experience tells us that there are two consistent ways of checking such tendencies. First, democratization of organizations and widening of their membership base is essential since it distributes power and diffuses hierarchy. Second, explicit assertion and commitment to an ethic that rejects personal aggrandizement, and a firm stance in that direction should be built into the organization from the beginning. We in the women's movement need to show by example that it is possible to bring these ethics to the centre of public life. Our own life experiences of powerlessness, cooperation, and nurturance can be enriching to our organizations, and to the world in which they function.

We do not claim to know all the answers to the problems, nor that there are unique solutions to them. In fact, we would assert that the solutions have to be worked out at the local level by the groups themselves. It is also important to recognize the cultural specificity of research methods and, especially, action. These depend on the social and cultural characteristics of regions and groups, though in general, women's groups appear more likely to be nonviolent and concerned about hierarchy and democratic processes. We need a great deal more self-understanding and dialogue about our own methods, problems, and successes in building organizations and managing power during the Decade, so that we can move ahead. Respect for the many voices of our movement, for their cross-fertilizing potential, for the power of dialogue, for the humility to learn from the experiences of others are crucial to our vision.

In many ways this book is the product of just such an ongoing process. Women from all over the globe and from many activities and professions have given unstintingly of their knowledge and experience through discussions, comments, criticisms, and suggestions. The process was always supportive even when it was critical or challenging. This speaks volumes for what we have learned is our most precious asset: the rich diversity of our experiences, understandings, and ideologies combined with a growing recognition that we cannot propose a social/political/economic programme for women alone, but that we need to develop one *for society from women's perspectives*. Thus, although the Decade that proclaimed so bravely "Development, Equality, Peace" has given so little of these to the majority of people, what we have learned in its course has already empowered us for the long haul ahead.

Notes

1 See *Development Dialogue* (1982), special issue, "Another Development with Women," for the proceedings of a symposium devoted to this theme, Jain, D. (1983), and Beneria and Sen (1981).
2 For similar perspectives on feminism, see the AAWORD Newsletter, *Feminism in Africa*, vol. II/III (1985), published by the Association of African Women for Research and Development; and *Bringing the Global Home, Feminism in the '80s – Book III* by Charlotte Bunch.
3 By now it should be clear that we use the term "Third World" as a positive self-affirmation based on our struggles against the multiple oppressions of nation, gender, class, and ethnicity.
4a See the "Report of the International Workshop on Feminist Ideology and Structures in the First Half of the Decade for Women," Bangkok, Thailand, June 1979, and "Report of the International Feminist Workshop" held at Stony Point, New York, April 1980.
4 We have the example of the U.S. where the gains made by the women's movement for equality in the 1970s left the core of the economic inequity untouched; in fact many of these gains were rolled back in the economic and political crunch of the 1980s, even though major changes in consciousness have occurred.
5 See El Saadawi (1980).
6 See Sen in RRPE (1984).
7 See Beneria (1982) and a number of the working papers and publications of the ILO's Rural Employment Programme as well as the Institute of Development Studies, Sussex.
8 See documents A/CONF.94/1–30 of the World Conference for the U.N. Decade for Women, 1980 and A/CONF.116/PC/21 of same, 1985, as well as Sivard (1985).
9 The writings emanating from the structuralist and dependency schools in Latin America, and from UNCTAD offer the best examples.
10 See Baran (1959) for a now classic statement of this argument.
11 See Chaudhuri (1982) and Palmer and Parsons (1977) for a few examples.
12 See Etienne and Leacock (1980) and Beneria and Sen (1981).
13 Boserup (1970) discusses the impact of colonialism in Chapter 3.
14 See Gonzalez (1984). The connections between gender subordination, racism, ethnic, and caste oppression in the Third World need to be studied more closely. There is a serious gap in research in this area.

15 See Ballance, Ansari and Singer (1982).

16 Both the World Bank and the IMF argue the merits of an export-oriented strategy that will lead to increases in both non-traditional and traditional exports in line with the factor endowments of a country.

17 See Ballance, Ansari and Singer (1982) for details.

18 See Burbach and Flynn (1980) for the details of the shift of pineapple cultivation from Hawaii to the Philippines in response to growing organization among agricultural labourers in Hawaii.

19 See Arizpe and Aranda (1981).

20 Williams (forthcoming) has a fascinating account of the origins of rural unrest in Central America consequent on appropriation of large areas for export crops and cattle ranching.

21 See Barnet and Muller (1974), and Girvan, Bernal and Hughes (1980) for the history of Jamaica's attempt to increase its share of bauxite revenues from the aluminium multinationals.

22 It is now well known that multinational corporations shift their production sites to Third World countries not only in search of cheap labour, raw materials or markets, but also to evade stringent anti-pollution or occupational safety requirements. See *Multinational Monitor*, various issues. The case of Union Carbide in Bhopal (India) or of the chemical companies that have created massive pollution problems in Puerto Rico under "Operation Bootstrap" are only two of a large number.

23 This is the perspective the World Bank espouses in its writings and tries to embed in its projects. For details of such a position by country, see the country series, *Foreign Trade Regimes and Economic Development* published by the National Bureau of Econonic Research, New York.

24 See Bhagwati and Desai (1970) for such a critique of India's import substitution programme.

25 By inward-oriented we mean strategies that emphasize production based primarily on internally-controlled capital and other resources for the domestic market. Disarticulation implies that different branches of producton are not well-linked to each other within the domestic economy, but may be more closely tied to the international economy.

26 See Fishlow (1972) and (1980) for an examination of the impact of Brazil's economic boom on the distribution of income.

27 See U.N. Cepal (1982) and Traverso and Iglesias (1983) for a discussion of the complex structural problems underpinning the Latin American economic crisis.

28 See Lee (1979) for a discussion of the Korean agrarian reform and de Janvry (1981).

29 Dore and Weeks (1982) have provided considerable evidence on this.

30 This is not necessarily an argument for collective or state farms; the recent experience of a number of countries raises questions about the organizational and managerial requirements of collective farming.

31 See Palmer and Parsons (1977) for examples from Central and Southern Africa.

Notes /99

32 In 1974, an inter-governmental commission jointly declared that food self-reliance was a prime necessity in the Sahel. See also the statements of the World Food Programme.

33 Both the IMF and the World Bank have explicitly supported structural adjustment programmes where "openness" of the economy is a condition for receiving funds.

34 For instance, in GATT trade negotiations, the U.S. government has pressured to have "services" (i.e., flows of profits, interest, royalties, etc.) become a major subject for negotiation, while Third World countries are more concerned about the growing protectionist barriers against their exports.

35 See Agarwal (1981) for a review of the literature.

36 See Tadesse (1982), Deere (1984) and Palmer (forthcoming) for cases from Ethiopia and Latin America.

37 See Sen (1985a) for details.

38 See Stoler (1977) for the example of rice cultivation in Java.

39 Mukhopadhyay (1983) discusses the decline of women's income from hand-pounding rice in Bengal in the 20th Century.

40 Muntemba (1982) and Bukh (1979) provide case studies of Zambia and Ghana. See also Okeyo (1980).

41 See Cecelski (1984) for the impact of the rural energy crisis on women.

42 See Heyzer (1982) and Elson and Pearson (1981) for an analysis of Southeast Asia.

43 Banerjee (1984) discusses this in depth.

44 Phongpaichit (1982) shows how the "informal" sector for women ranges from sweatshops to brothels.

45 Banerjee (1984), page 17.

46 Mies (1980) discusses lace-making for export under a putting-out system.

47 See Banerjee (1984) and U.N. Economic Commission for Africa (1984).

48 The U.N. Decade's evaluations show that, if anything, women's participation in this sector has increased as a result of the slowing down of economic growth and world trade during the last 10 years. See U.N. Economic Commission for Africa (1984b) and U.N. Economic Commission for Latin America and the Caribbean (1984).

49 See Heyzer (1981) for a discussion of the conceptual issues.

50 See U.N. Economic Commission for Africa (1984b).

51 See Ahmad (1984) and the ILO series, "Identification of Successful Projects for Improving the Employment Conditions of Rural Women" (1984), as well as Ellis in *Planning for Women in Rural Development*, (1984), pp. 84–92.

52 Oral evidence fom activists and organizers testifies to this. See Jain, S. (1984) for a well-documented case.

53 For example, it has been estimated that 80 percent of women in Ghana, and over 60 percent in Nigeria and Benin are traders, from small-scale to merchant enterprises. See U.N.E.C.A. (1984b), page 18.

54 Estimates for employment in this sector tend to err on the low side because of the presence of unpaid family labour (often female) that may not be counted.

55 See Poleman (1981) for a summary of the debate on the measurement of nutritional status.

56 See Mellor and Johnston (1984) and UNICEF (1984).

57 There is some difference between the approach to basic needs adopted by the ILO and the World Bank. The former tends to stress the importance of people's participation in project formulation and implementation, while the latter often seems to emphasize more the financial viability of the project, and "privatization" of operations. See ILO (1976) and McNamara (1973).

58 See Williams, G., (1981), Stryker (1979), Feder, (1977), de Alcantara (1976), and Mason and Asher (1973).

59 See Burgess (1978) and Payer (1982).

60 See Guha (1983), Shiva et al (1981), and Shiva and Bandopadhyay (1983) for discussions of deforestation and social forestry.

61 See *Development Dialogue*, 1980:2 on "The International Monetary System and the New International Order."

62 As stated in footnote 37, the ILO's programmes are somewhat of an exception.

63 Jain, L.C. (1984) has an elaborate discussion of the Indian government's switch to bureaucratically administered "integrated rural development programmes."

64 Unrest and rebellion in Central America have been traced to long term land alienation as a result of commercial cropping (Williams, forthcoming). In the short run, almost everywhere that the IMF has imposed a "structural adjustment" programme to reduce domestic demand by cutting real incomes (via subsidies for mass consumption items like bread, mass transit, health care, etc.) there have been riots, particularly in the urban areas. Sudan is the most recent example of this.

65 See Helzner (1984) for a recent discussion.

66 See Jain, L.C. (1984).

67 There is a growing suspicion among grassroots activists that large amounts of the resources flowing in response to the United Nations Decade on Water and Sanitation are being spent without adequate planning or local participation, and that there is therefore likely to be considerable "leakage."

68 See Jackson (1985). The information on this project is drawn from Jackson's case study and her reviews of additional evaluations of the Kano River Project.

69 Project evaluations selected for this review included the U.N. Voluntary Fund for Women Assessment (1984), Carloni (1983), Woodford-Berger (1983), McPhee (1982), Austin et al (1982), UNFPA (1985), Buvinic (1984), Pathfinder Fund documents (1983), Hartfiel (1982), Population Council and WAND (1984), and the Women's Roles and Gender Development: Cases for Planners Series, (1985) among others.

70 See Dey, J. (1984).

71 The findings of a number of consultants to donor agencies support this point. See Carloni (1983), Hartfiel (1982), PPCO/DIESA (1985).

72 See especially Hartfiel (1982).

73 See U.N.V.F.W. (1984), Carloni (1983), IPPF (1982), and McPhee (1982).

74 See U.N.V.F.W. (1984). While most of the Fund's projects experienced these kind of difficulties, the outlook is not entirely negative. A number of others proved more successful in terms of outcomes and participation of local women and could therefore serve as models for other agencies.

75 The case study undertaken by Harris-Williams in *Planning for Women in Rural Development* (1984) illustrates an example of an integrated rural development project in Jamaica that had negative results for the farmers in the community, but also had a relatively successful women's component.

76 See McPhee (1982), Carloni (1983), and Woodford-Berger (1983) for a discussion of checklist projects.

77 See Meek's (1971) introduction.

78 See Cain (1984), Caldwell (1983), and Nag (1977).

79 The data linking fertility status with women's education is usually presented in the form of simple correlations, without testing for the cross-effects of income, land-holding or mesaures of women's autonomy.

80 See *World Development Report* (1984), page 132.

81 See Pettigrew (1984) for the experiences of poor women with sterilization in the Punjab. Also see Shatrugna (no date).

82 For example, in India, female sterilizations (either post-partum or in sterilization camps) have become the dominant method of birth control. While vasectomy accounted for 89.5% of all sterilizatons in 1966–67, there has been a steady increase in tubectomies. By 1980–81, the latter accounted for 78.6% of all sterilizations done that year. See Shatrugna (no date), pp. 53–54. One suspects that the trend toward female-oriented techniques is a substitute for raising male consciousness. Many of the techniques now being proposed for use in the Third World, e.g., injectables, hormone implants, etc., have not received adequate safety testing.

83 The global struggle over infant formula provides a good analogy.

84 A crisis in the world economy or world trade can sometimes improve the situation of local people provided they still retain access to some land or other resources with which they can supply their needs. For example, large landowners may be more willing to allow land to be used for subsistence food if the market price for the cash crop has fallen. But for those who are full-time employees, economic downturn usually means increased misery.

85 See Fishlow (1970) for the case of Brazil.

86 Sri Lanka has been generally acclaimed for having achieved high levels of basic needs fulfilment during the 1960s despite low per capita incomes. So also the state of Kerala in India – see Centre for Development Studies (1974). Other societies like Nicaragua have given priority to basic needs, but face external pressures that are forcing a diversion of resources to defense.

87 Egypt is among a number of countries that faced such pressures after open door policies were initiated.

88 Jamaica, Egypt, the Dominican Republic, Peru, Brazil, Mexico are among a few recent examples.

89 This section draws heavily on Sen (1985b).

90 "From 1961–65 to 1973–77, the net imports of staple foods of developing countries increased nearly fivefold, from 5 to 23 million tons per year." (Mel-

lor, 1984, page 536).

91 See Morgan (1980) for a discussion of the world grain trade.

92 It is not clear how much the setting up of the IMP Cereal Import Facility has helped. See Adams (1983) for a discussion.

93 For example, in the poor states of Orissa, Bihar, and Karnataka in India, grain production stagnated during the 1970s even as national grain production was increasing. See Government of India, *Bulletin on Food Statistics*, various issues.

94 See de Alcantara (1976) for a Mexican example.

95 Given the higher population density and greater landlessness especially in South Asia, it is a matter of debate whether a redistributive land reform will provide viable holdings to the agricultural population. This makes rural and urban employment creation all the more important.

96 See Wijkman and Timberlake (1984), pp. 47–48.

97 According to Wijkman and Timberlake (1984), despite such a policy resolution, less than 40 percent of the $7.5 billion given as aid between 1975 and 1980 went to the rural areas. This was in part because peasants lacked political muscle, and in part because the technology for growing sorghum and millet on arid lands is still not very advanced.

98 See Wijkman and Timberlake (1984), page 35.

99 Despite past experiences, Zambia is currently approaching agencies for aid to construct 10 large dams in the southern maize-growing area, to be followed by others. While this may increase cereal and root-crop production by 5–6 times, it also threatens extensive damage to the land productivity if the dams are poorly designed and managed. See *The Hindu*, February 11, 1985, page 5.

100 For example, Kerala in southern India – a state known traditionally for its garden lands and ample perennial water supplies drawn from small streams and ponds that are replenished by seasonal rainfall – has begun to experience severe water shortages in years of inadequate rain. It is now being recognized that the effects of poor rainfall are considerably worsened by the rapid and alarming denudation of forests in the high ranges for industrial uses. Denudation is also occurring in the once lushly wooded slopes of the Himalayan foothills, and in the Andean countries (Bolivia, Ecuador, Peru, and Venezuela), along with significant dangers of desertification in Chile, Argentina, Mexico, and Peru. In many areas, such deforestation started in the colonial period.

101 See Cecelski (1984).

102 Wijkman and Timberlake, op.cit., pp. 122.

103 See Muntemba (1982) and Okeyo (1980).

104 See Cecelski (1984).

105 See Sen and Sen (1984).

106 See Bukh (1979).

107 See Batliwala (1982).

108 See Carloni (1981).

109 See Jain, S. (1984) for a discussion of the Chipko movement in India.

110 Wisner (1984) discusses the strengths of such groups.

111 The ORSTOM report on these recommendations and others is forthcoming.

112 Block (1977) has an informative discussion of the opposing interests that went into the formation of the Bretton Woods System.

113 See Traverso and Iglesias (1983) and various issues of the CEPAL Review.

114 de Janvry and Ground (1978) dissect the experience with land reform in Latin Amercia under the Alliance for Progress.

115 Transfer-pricing is when one subsidiary of a multinational corporation sells to another subsidiary at artificially high or artificially low prices for greater financial gain. For an account of how these intracorporate transfers work, see Caves (1982) and Quirin (1979).

116 Refer to Traverso and Iglesias (1983).

117 See *World Development* (1980) for a special issue on economic stabilization.

118 See Dell in *World Development* (1980), and Dell and Lawrence (1980), among others. Interestingly the case for sharing the burden is vociferously argued by the U.S. and Western Europe against Japanese trade surpluses.

119 See Thorp and Whitehead (1977) for a number of case studies.

120 India with its strongly inward-oriented industrialization offers a counterexample. Up till the late 1970s, Indian policy toward private direct investment and to commercial borrowing remained quite conservative so that debt service as a percentage of exports of goods and services in 1981 was only 7.1 percent (*World Development Report*, 1984). This ratio is likely to increase because of higher commercial borrowing and a large loan taken under the IMF's Extended Fund Facility in 1981.

121 See Dore and Weeks (1982) for the evidence on Chile after 1973. Also see Cline and Weintraub (1981) and Dell and Lawrence (1980).

122 See U.N. Secretariat (1981).

123 Refer Banerjee (1984).

124 See Prates (1981).

125 See U.N. Secretariat (1981) for the examples of Chile and Sri Lanka.

126 The Latin American preparatory meeting for the NGO Forum (to be held along with the U.N. Decade for Women Conference in Nairobi, July 1985) at Havana in November 1984 strongly endorsed the need for such research.

127 The steep rise in military spending has also contributed, along with the tax cuts, to the record increases in the federal budget deficit (larger than the total of all deficits for the previous 20 years). The national deficit is now so big that interest payments on it have soared to over $100 billion a year – which is more than the combined cost of all low income programmes in the entire federal budget. See Adams (1983) and Center on Budget and Policy Priorities (1984).

128 See Center on Budget and Policy Priorities (1984), Sparr (1984), Palmer and Sawhill (1984).

129 Ibid.

130 Black and Hispanic unemployment levels have not declined as much as white unemployment levels and remain higher than they were before the recession began.

131 See Noyelle (1985), Applebaum (1985), and Sassen-Koob (1985) for analyses

of long-term structural transformations in the U.S. economy. Refer to Mattera (1985) for an account of the rise of the "informal sector" in the U.S.

132 Some examples from Latin America include the Casa da Mulher in Sao Paulo, Brazil, Flora Tristan and Peru Mujer in Lima, Peru, and the Casa de la Mujer in Colombia.

133 See United Nations A/36/356 (1982) and A/37/386 (1983) and Sivard (1983), p. 19.

134 In 1983, the number of refugees was estimated at 8 million, although many believe this understates the total. See Sivard (1983), p. 19.

135 Military expenditure estimates by Sivard exclude verterans' benefits, interest on war debts, civilian defense, outlays for strategic industrial stockpiling, national intelligence expenditures and tax-exemptions for military property.

136 U.N. (1983), op.cit., p. 8.

137 The six main military spenders are the U.S., the U.S.S.R., China, France, the U.K., and West Germany. It should be noted that there are significant differences within this group. Not all are leading in the process of arms innovation or in the production and export of arms; military expenditure (particularly per capita) differs widely within the group, and not all have military capability that give them a global military-strategic importance. In addition to these countries, the U.N. reported that other nations such as Israel have emerged as large arms exporters, particularly to military-dominated or repressive regimes in the Third World. By 1980, for example, South Africa had become the largest single customer of arms exported by Israel's arms exports. South Africa alone imported more arms than all the other African states combined throughout the 1950s and 1960s.

138 See U.N. (1983), op.cit. A host of political and strategic considerations often accompany commercial arms transactions. The actual terms of transfer deals are rarely made public, but according to the U.N., they include concessional modes of payment, periods of delivery, supply of spare parts and supportive equipment, arrangements for colicensing, co-production and training facilities for handling the equipment. Military assistance programmes, training courses for military personnel, provisions for military bases, naval facilities and listening posts, and tacit and explicit understandings for political and military support in situations of internal unrest, are arrangements known to go along with weapons imports.

139 Sivard's *World Military and Social Expenditures*, 1981, 1982, 1983 provide the data cited in this section.

140 See U.N. (1983), op.cit., p. 7.

141 See the studies by Adams (1982), Melman (1983), Hartung (1984), Anderson (1982), DeGrasse (1983), and Leontief and Duchin (1983).

142 See Sivard (1982), p. 18 and the 1983 report of the U.S. Congressional Budget Office.

143 See Sivard (1983), p. 24.

144 See Kitchenman (1983) or the Rand Corporation checklist (July 1984) for a summary of his study.

145 See Sivard (1982), p. 9 and (1983) p. 16.

146 See Anderson (1982) and Sivard (1981).

147 See Sivard (1982), p. 19.

148 DeGrasse (1982) and Sivard (1981), p. 19 found that in 17 and 10 developed countries respectively for which historical data are available, growth in investment and in manufacturing productivity was negatively correlated with the share of military expenditure in GNP. However this simple correlation may well be a spurious one.

149 See Sivard (1982), p. 7.

150 See *Dollars and Sense*, No. 98, July/August 1984, p. 14.

151 See Sivard (1981), p. 16.

152 Helleiner (1984) discusses the growing neglect of the poorest countries in share of aid and financial liquidity.

153 See Leontief and Duchin (1983).

154 Sivard's classificaton of military ruled governments includes both those that result from coups and those that result from popular struggles.

155 Amnesty International is the major source of information in this area.

156 See Williams (forthcoming).

157 Right-wing death squads are well known to be associated with and often to include members of the military and paramilitary forces.

158 ITT's involvement in the Chilean coup of 1973 is widely suspected.

159 The rapid rise of Le Pen in recent years in France's political right is an example. Le Pen explicitly blames North African workers for unemployment and calls for their expulsion from France; he is only the latest of a number of such politicians in Europe.

160 See Afshar (1985) for details of the effects of the Iranian theocracy on women.

161 Gilder (1981) blames both women and blacks for high unemployment levels in the U.S.

162 See Afshar (no date).

163 See Bridenthal, Grossman, and Kaplan (1985).

164 Youth unemployment and the search for national values also fuel the growth of religious fundamentalism, as has been happening in Egypt and Morocco. The effects of an age-structure tending towards youth can be explosive in a situation of mass unemployment and underemployment, because the aspirations of the young turn to frustration, anger and despair.

165 Khomeini was exiled by the Shah for opposing changes in women's civil status – this is a little known fact.

166 The examples of Sistren in the Caribbean and Stree Mukti Sanghatana in India are only two of many.

167 See Bhasin and Agarwal (1984) for an analysis of an alternatives to women's current portrayal in the media.

168 Thus UNICEF provided funding that allowed Stree Mukti Sanghatana to tour a number of towns in India in 1984 with street theatre, music, and discussion sessions.

169 See Accelerated Development in Sub-Saharan Africa: "An Agenda for Action" written by Dr. Elliot Berg in 1981 for the World Bank; the Lagos Plan

of Action for the Implementation of the Monrovia Strategy for the Economic Development of Africa adopted by the OAU in 1980; and Shepard, J. (1985) for an interesting account of the Reagan Administration's development assistance policy in Africa.

170 A number of examples of women pooling their resources and operating soup kitchens, for example, exist in Brazil, Colombia, and Mexico.

171 Examples of such organizations include the worldwide YWCAs, the All India Women's Congress, Associated Countrywomen of the World, and the National Council of Women's Societies in Nigeria, among others.

172 The Self Employed Women's Association (SEWA) and the Working Women's Forum in India, Makulamada in Sri Lanka, as well as 9 to 5 in the U.S. are some examples of the types of existing worker-based organizations. The ILO has also documented a number of women's initiatives in worker organizations in all regions of the world. Ahmad (1984), for example, describes the Malaysian Trade Congress and the women's initiative in Pem, which started a centre for training and education of women trade union members.

173 In Latin America, the Casa da Mulher (São Paulo, Brazil) works on self help issues and sex education, SOS Mulher (Recife, Brazil) and Casa de la Mujer (Colombia), focus on domestic violence. Flora Tristan (Lima, Peru) gives legal aid, and Peru Mujer (Lima, Peru) helps to develop women's skills. Grassroots women's organizations in other areas of the world include: the Gonoshashtyo Kendra (Bangladesh), the Women's Resource Center (Papua New Guinea), and the Muvman Liberasian Fam in Mauritius. See the newsletter, resource guides, and other publications of the International Women's Tribune Center in New York for more examples of this type of organization.

174 AAWORD (Senegal), AWRAN (Asia), WAND (Caribbean), PAWF (Asia/Pacific), ALCEA (Central/Latin-America), and the Institute for Women's Studies in the Arab World (Mid-East) are regional research and action networks which have grown in the last 10 years.

175 The Alliance Against Sex Tourism (Southeast Asia and the Pacific), the Greenbelt Movement (Kenya), the Chipko Movement (India), the Infant Formula Action Coalition (INFACT), and the Black and Favelas Movement (Brazil) all come under the rubric of the movements described here.

176 For a description of the Mexico Coalition that formed around the issues of rape, abortion, and women's rights at work, see the Report of the International Feminist Workshop held at Stony Point, New York, April 1980. Other such networks and coalitions include CARIWA in the Caribbean, ISIS International, and the International Feminist Network Against the Trafficking of Women.

Bibliography

1 Adams, G., *Controlling Weapons Costs: Can the Pentagon Reforms Work?*, New York, Council on Economic Priorities, 1983
2 Adams, G., *The Politics of Defense Contracting: The Iron Triangle*, New Jersey, Transaction Book, 1982.
3 Adams, R., "The Role of Research in Policy Development: the Creation of the IMF Cereal Import Facility," *World Development*, 11:7, July 1983, pp. 549–63.
4 Afshar, H., (ed) *Iran, a Revolution in Turmoil*, London, Macmillian, 1985.
5 Afshar, H., "Women, State and Ideology in Iran," unpublished manuscript, no date.
6 Agarwal, B., "Agricultural Modernization and Third World Women," Geneva, ILO, May 1981.
7 Ahmad, Z. "Rural Women, Their Conditions of Work and Struggle to Organize," Geneva, ILO, November 1984
8 Ahmad, Z., "The Plight of Rural Women: Alternatives for Action," Geneva, *International Labour Review*, July-August 1980.
9 Anderson, M., *The Empty Pork Barrel: Unemployment and the Pentagon Budget*, Michigan, Employment Research Associates, 1982
10 APCWD, "Report of the International Workshop on Feminist Ideology and Structures in the First Half of the Decade for Women," Bangkok, Thailand, June 1979.
11 Applebaum, E., "Technology and the Reorganization of Work", unpublished manuscript, march 1985.
12 Arizpe, L. and Aranda, J., "The Comparative Advantages of Women's Disadvantages: Women Workers in the Strawberry Export Agri-Business in Mexico," *Signs-Journal of Women in Culture and Society*, 7:2, Winter 1981.
13 Aspin, L. (Congressman), "Defense Spending and the Economy," U.S. House of Representatives, Washington, D.C., April 1984.
14 Austin, J., Anderson, M.B., Cloud, K., and Overholt, C., "Guidelines for the Preparation of Case Studies on Women in Development," paper prepared for the Office of Women in Development of USAID, Washington D.C., April 1982.
15 Azad, N. et al, "Improving Working Conditions for Rural Women Through Creation of Alternative Employment Options: A Case Study of the Working Women's Forum," Rural Employment Policies branch, ILO, Geneva, 1984.

16 Ballance, R., Ansari, J., and Singer, H., *The International Economy and Industrial Development*, Brighton, Harvester Press, 1982.

17 Banerjee, N., "Women and Industrialization in Developing Countries," unpublished manuscript, 1984 (eds).

18 Banerjee, N. and Jain, D., (eds) *Tyranny of the Household*, New Delhi, Vikas Publishers, 1985a.

19 Baran, P.A., *The Political Economy of Growth*, New York, Monthly Review Press, 1959.

20 Barroso, C. and Schmink, M., "Women's Programs for the Andean Region and the Southern Cone: Assessment and Recommendations," New York, Ford Foundation, March 1984.

21 Barnet, R., and Muller, R., *Global Reach: The Power of the Multinational Corporations*, New York, Simon and Schuster, 1974.

22 Batliwala, S., "Rural Energy Scarcity and Nutrition: A New Perspective," *Economic and Political Weekly*, (XVII, 1982, p. 329)

23 Beneria, L., and Sen, G., "Accumulation, Reproduction and Women's Role in Economic Development: Boserup Revisited," *Signs-Journal of Women in Culture and Society* 7:2, Winter 1981, pp. 279–298.

24 Beneria, L. (ed) *Women and Development – the Sexual Division of Labour in Rural Societies*, New York, Praeger/ILO, 1982.

25 Berg, E., "Accelerated Development in Sub-Saharan Africa: An Agenda for Research and Action," a World Bank report, Washington, D.C., 1981.

26 Bhagwati, J. and Desai, P., *India – Planning for Industrialization*, London, Oxford University Press, 1970.

27 Bhasin, K. and Agarwal, B., *Women and Media*, New Delhi, Kali for Women, 1984.

28 Bleie, T. and Lund, R., (eds) *Gender Relations: The Missing Link in the Development Puzzle, A Selected and Annotated Bibliographic Guide to Theoretical Efforts and South Asian Experiences*, DERAP Publications No. 184, Norway, The Christian Michelsen Institute, March 1985.

29 Block, F., *The Origins of International Economic Disorder*, Berkeley, University of California Press, 1977.

30 Bose, M., Loufti, M., and Muntemba, S., "Rural Development with Women: Elements of Success," paper prepared for the African and Asian Interregional ILO Workshop on "Strategies for Improving the Employment Conditions of Rural Women," Tanzania, August 1984.

31 Boserup, E., *Women's Role in Economic Development*, London, Allen and Unwin, 1970.

32 Bridenthal, R., Grossman, A., and Kaplan, M., (eds) *When Biology Became Destiny: Women in Weimar and Nazi Germany*, New York, Monthly Review Press, 1985.

33 Bridges, W.P., "Industry Marginality and Female Employment: A New Appraisal," *American Sociological Review*, February 1980, pp. 58–75.

34 Bukh, J., *The Village Women in Ghana*, Uppsala, Scandinavian Institute of African Studies, 1979.

35 Burfisher, M. and Horenstein, N., "Sex Role in the Nigerian TIV Farm

Household," in Women's Roles and Gender Differences in Development: Cases for Planners Series, Connecticut, Kumarian Press, 1985.

36 Burbach, R. and Flynn, P., *Agribusiness in the Americas*, New York, Monthly Review Press, 1980.

37 Burgess, R., "Petty Commodity Housing or Dweller Control? A Critique of John Turner's Views on Housing Policy," *World Development*, 6:9/10, September-October, 1978.

38 Buvinic, M., "Projects for Women in the Third World: Explaining Their Misbehavior," Washington, D.C., International Centre for Research on Women, April 1984.

39 Cain, M. "Women's Status and Fertility in Developing Countries: Son Preference and Economic Security," World Bank Staff Working Papers 682, 1984.

40 Caldwell, J., "A Theory of Fertility: From High Plateau to Destabilization," *Population and Development Review* 9:1, March 1983

41 Carloni, A., "Integrating Women in Agricultural Projects: Case Studies of Ten FAO Assisted Field Projects," Rome, FAO, 1983.

42 Carloni, A.S., "Sex Disparities in the Distribution of Food Within Rural Households," *Food and Nutrition* 7:1, 1981.

43 Caves, R., *Multinational Enterprise and Economic Analysis*, New York, Cambridge University Press, 1982.

44 Cecelski, E., "The Rural Energy Crisis, Women's Work and Family Welfare: Perspectives and Approaches to Action," Geneva, ILO WEP Working Paper, June 1984.

45 Centre for Development Studies, *Poverty, Unemployment and Development Policy*, United Nations, New York, 1974.

46 Center on Budget and Policy Priorities, *End Results: The Impact of Federal Policies Since 1980 on Low-Income Americans*, Washington, D.C., September 1984.

47 Chaudhuri, B., "Agrarian Relations – Eastern India" in *The Cambridge Economic History of India*, Vol. II, Cambridge University Press, 1982, pp. 86–176.

48 Children's Defense Fund, *American Children in Poverty*, Washington, D.C., 1984.

49 Children's Defense Fund, *A Children's Defense Budget: An Analysis of the President's Budget and Children*, Washington, D.C., 1985.

50 Cline, W.R. and Weintraub, S. (eds), *Economic Stabilization in Developing Countries*, Washington, D.C., Brookings Institution, 1981.

51 Commission on the Status of Women, "Forward-Looking Strategies of Implementation for the Advancement of Women and Concrete Measures to Overcome Obstacles to the Achievements of the Goals and Objectives of the United Nations Decade for Women," A/CONF.116/PC/21, Vienna, December 1984.

52 Congressional Budget Office, *Defense Spending and the Economy*, Washington, D.C., U.S. Government Printing Office, February 1983.

53 Das Gupta, B. and Connell, J., *Migration from Rural Areas: The Evidence from Village Studies*, New Delhi, Oxford University Press, 1976.

54 de Alcantara, C.H., *Modernizing Mexican Agriculture: Socioeconomic Implications of Technological Change, 1940–1970*, Geneva, UNRISD, 1976.

55 Deere, C.D., "Rural Women and State Policy: The Latin American Agrarian Reform Experience," unpublished manuscript, October 1984.

56 DeGrasse, R., *The Costs and Consequences of Reagan's Military Build-up, A Report to the IAM and the Coalition for a New Foreign and Military Policy*, New York, Council on Economic Priorities, 1982.

57 DeGrasse, R., *Military Expansion, Economic Decline*, New York, M.I. Sharpe, Inc., 1983.

58 de Janvry, A., and Ground, L., "Types and Consequences of Land Reform in Latin America," *Latin American Perspectives* V:4, Fall 1978, pp. 90–112.

59 de Janvry, A., *The Agrarian Question and Reformism in Latin America*, Baltimore, The Johns Hopkins University Press, 1981.

60 Dey, J., "Women in Food Production and Food Security in Africa," Women in Agriculture Series   3, Rome, FAO, 1984.

61 Dell, S. and Lawrence, R., *The BOP Adjustment Process in Developing Countries*, London, Pergamon Policy Studies, 1980.

62 *Development Dialogue*, "The International Monetary System and the New International Order," 1980:2.

63 *Development Dialogue*, "Another Development with Women," 1982:1/2.

64 *Dollars and Sense*, a publication of the Economic Affairs Bureau, Boston, Massachusetts, various issues 1982-present.

65 Dore, E.W. and Weeks, J.F., "Economic Performance and Basic Needs: the Examples of Brazil, Chile, Mexico, Nicaragua, Peru and Venezuela," in *Human Rights and Basic Needs in the Americas*, Washington, D.C., Georgetown University Press, 1982, pp. 150–187.

66 Eisold, E., "Young Women Workers in Export Industries: The Case of the Semiconductor Industry in Southeast Asia," WEP Research Working Papers, Geneva, ILO, March 1984.

67 El Saadawi, N., *The Hidden Face of Eve: Women in the Arab World*, Boston, Beacon Press, 1980.

68 Elson, D. and Pearson, R., "Nimble Fingers Make Cheap Workers: An Analysis of Women's Employment in Third World Export Manufacturing," *Feminist Review*, Spring 1981, pp. 87–107.

69 Etienne, M. and Leacock, E., *Women and Colonization*, New York, Praeger, 1980.

70 Feder, E., "Capitalism's Last-Ditch Effort to Save Underdeveloped Agricultures: International Agribusiness, the World Bank and the Rural Poor," *Journal of Contemporary Asia* 7:1, 1977, pp. 56–78.

71 Fishlow, A., "The Brazilian Size Distribution of Income," *American Economic Review* LX II:2, May 1972, pp. 391–402.

72 Fishlow, A., "Who Benefits from Economic Development? Comment," *American Economic Review* 70:1, March 1980, pp. 250–256.

73 Gilder, G., *Wealth and Poverty*, New York, Basic Books, 1981.

74 Girvan, N., Bernal, R. and Hughes, W., "The IMF and the Third World: the Case of Jamaica, 1974–80," *Development Dialogue* 1980:2.

75 Gonzalez, L., "The Black Woman's Place in Brazilian Society," paper pre-

sented at *1985 and Beyond: A National Conference*, Morgan State University, Baltimore, August 1984.

76 Government of India, *Bulletin on Food Statistics*, various issues.

77 Guha, R., "Forestry in British and Post-British India: A Historical Analysis," *Economic and Political Weekly*, October 29 and November 5, 1983.

78 Hartfiel, A., "In Support of Women: Ten Years of Funding by the Inter-American Foundation," paper presented to the IAF Board of Directors, September 1982.

79 Hartung, W., *The Economic Consequences of a Nuclear Freeze*, New York, Council on Economic Priorities, New York, 1984.

80 Helleiner, G.K., "Aid and Liquidity: The Neglect of the Poorest in the Emerging International Monetary System," Round Table on International Monetary and Fiancial System and Issues, ICRIER, New Delhi, December 1984.

81 Helzner, J., "Bringing Women into People Centered Development," unpublished manuscript, November 1984.

82 Helzner, J., and Krueger, C., "Integrating Women: An Evaluation of the Women's Socioecnomic Participation Project," paper prepared for USAID, Washington, D.C., September 1984.

83 Heyzer, N., "Towards a Framework of Analysis," *IDS Bulletin* 12:3, July 1981 (Special Issue on Women and the Informal Sector).

84 Heyzer, N., "From Rural Subsistence to an Industrial Peripheral Work Force: An Examination of Female Malaysian Migrants and Capital Accumulation in Singapore," in Beneria (ed), 1982.

85 Hill, H., "Women, War and Third World Development," *Labour Forum*, a publication of the Australian Labour Party, S.A. Branch, 1984.

86 *Hindu*, Feb. 11, 1985.

87 ILO, "Asian and Pacific Case Studies: Summaries," paper prepared for Asian and Pacific Regional Workshop on Strategies for Improving the Employment Conditions of Rural Women, Malaysia, November 1983.

88 ILO, *Employment, Growth and Basic Needs: A One-World Problem*, New York, Prayer, 1976.

89 INSTRAW, "Final Report of Interregional Seminar on Women and the International Drinking Water Supply and Sanitation Decade"? INSTRAW/BT/1985/CRP.1, Dominican Republic, November 1984.

90 INSTRAW, "Report on the Expert Group Meeting on the Role of Women in New and Renewable Sources of Energy," Dominican Republic, 1985.

91 International Planned Parenthood Federation (IPPF), *Planned Parenthood and Women's Development: Lessons From the Field*, London, 1982.

92 Jackson, C., "Kano River Irrigation Project," in Women's Roles and Gender Differences in Development: Cases for Planners Series, Connecticut, Kumarian Press, 1985.

93 Jain, D., "Development as if Women Mattered or Can Women Build a New Paradigm?," lecture delivered at OECD/DAC Meeting, Paris, January 1983.

94 Jain, L.C., *Grass Without Roots*, New Delhi, Institute of Social Studies Trust, 1984.

95 Jain, S., "Women and People's Ecological Movement – A Case Study of

Women's Role in the Chipko Movement in Uttar Pradesh," *Economic and Political Weekly*, October 13, 1984.

96 Jones, L. and Il Sakong, *Government, Business and Entrepreneurship in Economic Development: the Korean Case*, Cambridge, Harvard University Press, 1980.

97 Kitchenman, W., *Arms Transfers and the Indebtedness of Less Developed Countries*, Rand Corporation Study, N-2O2O-FF, Santa Monica, California, 1983.

98 Kuhn, S. and Bluestone, B., "The New Economic Dualism: U.S. Women and the Transformation of the Global Economy," paper prepared for the conference on "Women and Structural Transformation: The Crisis of Work and Family Life," Rutgers University, New Jersey, November 1983.

99 Leacock, E., *Myths of Male Dominance*, New York, Monthly Review Press, 1981.

100 Lee, E., "Egalitarian Peasant Farming and Rural Development: The Case of South Korea," *World Development* 7:4–5, April-May 1979, pp. 493–517.

101 Leontief, W. and Duchin F. *Military Spending: Facts and Figures, Worldwide Implications and Future Outlook*, New York, Oxford University Press, 1983.

102 Lund, R., "Women and Development Planning in Sri Lanka," *Geografiska Annaler*, 63B, Norway, 1981.

103 Lund, R., "Women's Working and Living Conditions in a Mahaweli Settlement Area," *Economic Review*, Aug./Sept. 1979.

104 Mamdani, M., *The Myth of Population Control*, New York, Monthly Review Press, 1972.

105 MacCormack, C. and Strathern, M., *Nature, Culture and Gender*, London, Cambridge University Press, 1980.

106 Mason, E. and Asher, R., *The World Bank Since Bretton Woods*, Washington D.C., The Brookings Institution, 1973.

107 Mattera, P., *The Rise of the Underground Economy*, London Pluto Press, 1985.

108 McNamara, R., Address to the Board of Governors of the World Bank, Nairobi, 1973, Washington, D.C., World Bank, 1973.

109 McPhee, S., "The Checklist Project: Project Evaluation Techniques and Women's Contribution," SIDA, Stockholm, November 1982.

110 Meek, R.L., (ed) *Marx and Engels on the Population Bomb*, Berkeley, Rampart Press, 1971.

111 Mellor, J. and Johnston, B., "The World Food Equation: Interrelations Among Development, Employment and Food Consumption," *Journal of Economic Literature*, 222, June 1984.

112 Melman, S., *Profits Without Production*, New York, Alfred A. Knopf, 1983.

113 Mies, M., *The Lace-Makers of Narsapur: Housewives Produce for the World Market*, Geneva, ILO, 1980.

114 Mies, M., "Indian Women in Subsistence and Agricultural Labour," WEP Research Working Papers, Geneva, ILO, May 1984.

115 Morgan, D., *The Merchants of Grain*, New York, Penguin, 1980.

116 Mukhopadhyay, M., "The Impact of Modernization on Women's Occupa-

tions: A Case Study of the Rice Husking Industry of Bengal," *Indian Economic and Social History Review* XX:1, January-March, 1983, pp. 27–46.

117 Muntemba, S., "Women as Food Producers and Suppliers in the Twentieth Century: The Case of Zambia," *Development Dialogue*, 1982.

118 *Multinational Monitor*, Washington, D.C., various issues.

119 Nag, M., Peet, R. and White, B., "Economic Value of Children in Two Peasant Societies," International Population Conference, Mexico, 1977, Volume 1.

120 *New York Times*, "Debt Crisis Seen as Ending," Feb. 4, 1985.

121 Noyelle, T., "American Women Confront the New Technology and the New World Economy: Past Achievements and Future Challenges," paper prepared for the North American Workshop of the Society for International Development, April 1985.

122 Oakley, P. and Marsden, D., "Approaches to Participation in Rural Development," paper for Inter-Agency Panel on People's Participation, Geneva, ILO, March 1983.

123 Okeyo, A.P., "Daughters of the Lakes and Rivers: Colonization and the Land Rights of Luo women," in Etienne and Leacock (eds) 1980.

124 Okeyo, A.P., "Definitions of Women and Development: An African Perspective," in *Women and National Development: The Complexities of Change*, Chicago, University of Chicago Press, 1977.

125 Organization of African Unity (OAU), "The Lagos Plan of Action for the Implementation of the Monrovia Strategy for the Economic Development of Africa," 1980.

126 Palmer, J. and Sawhill, I., (eds) *The Reagan Record: An Urban Institute Study*, Massachusetts, Ballinger, 1984.

127 Palmer, I., "The Nemow Case," in Women's Roles and Gender Differences in Development: Cases for Planners Series, Connecticut, Kumarian Press, 1985.

128 Palmer, I., "The Impact of Agrarian Reform on Women," in Women's Roles and Gender Differences in Development: Cases for Planners Series, Connecticut, Kumarian Press, 1985.

129 Palmer, R., and Parsons, N., (eds) *The Roots of Rural Poverty in Central and Southern Africa*, Berkeley, University of California Press, 1977.

130 Payer, C., *The World Bank – A Critical Analysis*, New York, Monthly Review Press, 1982.

131 Pettigrew J., "Problems Concerning Tubectomy Operations in Rural Areas of Punjab," *Economic and Political Weekly* XIX:26, June 30, 1984, pp. 995–1002.

132 Phongpaichit, P., *From Peasant Girls to Bangkok Masseuses*, Geneva, ILO, 1982.

133 Poleman, T., "Quantifying the Nutrition Situation in Developing Countries," *Food Research Institute Studies* 18(1) 1981, pp. 1–58.

134 Population Council and WAND, University of the West Indies, *Planning for Women in Rural Development: A Source Book for the Caribbean*, Barbados, Coles Printery Limited, 1984.

135 PPCO/DIESA, "Cross Organizational Review of the Selected Major Issues

in the Medium Term Plans of the Organizations of the U.N. System," draft paper, New York, January 1985.

136 Prates, S., "Women's Labour and Family Survival Strategies Under the Stabilization Models in Latin America," Expert Group Meeting on Policies for Social Integration, CSDHA/UN, Vienna, September 1981.

137 Quirin, M., *Fiscal Transfer-Pricing in Multinational Corporations*, Toronto, University of Toronto Press, 1979.

138 Rand Corporation Checklist, Santa Monica, California, July 1984.

139 Sachs, K., *Sisters and Wives: The Past and Future of Sexual Equality*, Illinois, University of Illinois Press, 1979.

140 Sassen-Koob, S., "Notes on the Incorporation of Third World Women into Wage-Labour Through Immigration and Off-Shore Production," *International Migration Review*, Summer 1985.

141 Scott, H., *Working your Way to the Bottom: The Feminization of Poverty*, London, Pandora Press, 1984.

142 Sen, C. and Sen, G., "Women's Domestic Work and Economic Activity: Results from the National Sample Survey," paper presented at the workshop on Women in the Third World, CEDE Bogota, August 1984.

143 Sen, G., "Subordination and Sexual Control: A Comparative View of the Control of Women," in *Review of Radical Political Economics* 16:1, Spring 1984.

144 Sen, G., "Women Agricultural Labourers – Regional Variations in Incidence and Employment," Banerjee, N. and Jain, D. (eds), 1985a.

145 Sen, G., "Changing International Perspectives Towards Women and Food – An Appraisal," paper presented at the International Workshop on Women's Role in Food Self-Sufficiency and Food Strategies, ORSTOM/CIE, Paris, January 1985b.

146 Sen, S.K., "The Working Women in West Bengal: A Study of Popular Movements and Women's Organizations," paper prepared for the African and Asian Interregional ILO Workshop on Strategies for Improving Employment Conditions of Rural Women, Tanzania, August 1984.

147 Seth, N., "Choices Regarding Fertility Control in Developing Countries: Women-Centered Educational Perspectives," unpublished manuscript, December 1984.

148 Shatrugna, V., "Women and Health," *Current Information Series 2*, Research Unit on Women's Studies, S.N.D.T. Women's University, India, no date.

149 Shepard, J. "When Foreign Aid Fails," *The Atlantic*, 255:4, April 1985.

150 Shiva, V., Sharatchandra H.C. and Bandopadhyaya, J., *Social and Ecological Impact of Social Forestry in Kolar*, Bangalore, Indian Institute of Management, 1981.

151 Shiva, V. and Bandopadhyay, J., "Eucalyptus – A Disastrous Tree for India," *The Ecologist* 13:5, 1983.

152 Sivard, R., *World Military and Social Expenditures: An Annual Report on World Priorities*, Washington, D.C., 1980, 1981, 1982, 1983.

153 Sivard, R., *Women, A World Survey*, Washington, D.C., 1985.

154 Simmons, A., "The Value of Children Approach in Population Policies:

New Hope or False Promise," International Population Conference, Mexico, 1977, Volume 1.

155 Sparr, P., "Re-Evaluating Feminist Economics," *Dollars and Sense*, No. 99, September 1984.

156 Stjernstedt, D.C., "Success of Rural Women's Projects: Mumbwa Case Zambia," Rural Employment Policies Branch, Geneva, ILO, 1984.

157 Stoler, A., "Class Structure and Female Autonomy in Rural Java," *Signs – Journal of Women in Culture and Society* 3:1, Autumn, 1977, pp. 74–89.

158 Stryker, R., "The World Bank and Agricultural Development," *World Development* 7:3, March 1979.

159 Traverso, C.A. and Iglesias, E.V., *Basis for a Latin American Response to the International Economic Crisis*, SELA-ECLA, May 1983.

160 U.N. Cepal, "Latin American Development Problems and the World Economic Crisis," E/CEPAL/CEGAN 6/L.2, November 1982.

161 U.N. Economic Commission for Africa, "Review and Appraisal of the Achievements of the U.N. Decade for Women, 1976–1985," E/ECA/RCIWD/OAU/4, August 1984b.

162 U.N. Economic Commission for Africa, "Women and the Industrial Development Decade in Africa," E/ECA/RCIWD/OAU/6, August 1984.

163 U.N. Economic Commission for Latin America and the Caribbean, "Report of the Group of Experts on Operational Strategies for the Advancement of Women Up to the Year 2000," LC/G.1322, September 1984.

164 U.N. Centre for Disarmament, "The Relationship Between Disarmament and Development," Disarmament Study Series 5, A/36/356, New York, 1982.

165 U.N. Department for Disarmament Affairs, "Economic and Social Consequences of the Arms Race and of Military Expenditures," A/37/386, New York, 1983.

166 UNFPA Evaluation Branch, "Draft Guidelines for the Evaluation of Women's Role in UNFPA Assisted Programmes," New York, 1984.

167 UNICEF, *The State of the World's Children*, New York, 1984.

168 U.N. Secretariat, Branch for the Advancement of Women, "Resource Paper on Women in Developing Countries and Monetary and Fiscal Matters in the Context of the International Development Strategy," AWB/EGM,81.2/RP.4, November 1981.

169 U.N. Secretariat, World Conference of the United Nations Decade for Women Documents, A/CONF.94/1–30, New York, 1980.

170 U.N. Voluntary Fund for the United Nations Decade for Women, "Development Cooperation with Women: The Experience and Future Directions of the Fund," (preliminary report), IESA/SDHA/CC.16/3–6, New York, August 1984.

171 *Wall Street Journal*, February 17, 1985.

172 WAND and APCWD, "Developing Strategies for the Future: Feminist Perspectives," Report of the International Feminist Workshop held at Stony Point, New York, April 1980.

173 Women for Economic Justice, "When the Rich Get Richer and the Poor Get

Poorer, What Happens to Women and Children?" Economic Literacy
Paper   1, Boston, 1984.

174 Wijkman, A. and Timberlake, L., *Natural Disasters – Acts of God or Man?*,
London, Earthscan, 1984.

175 Williams, G., "The World Bank and the Peasant Problem," in *Rural Development in Tropical Africa* (eds) Heyer, J., Roberts, P., and Williams, G.,
London, Macmillan, 1981.

176 Williams, R., *Cotton, Cattle and Crisis in Central America*, North Carolina,
University of North Carolina Press, forthcoming.

177 Wisner, B., "Energy – Agriculture Conflicts and Complementarities in African Development: Experiences with Method," paper presented at the International Seminar on Ecosystems, Food and Energy, Brasilia, September
1984.

178 Woodford-Berger, P., "Monitoring Women: The Use of Checklists in Rural
Assistance Programmes Against the Background of Ten Case Studies,"
paper submitted to the OECD/DAC/WID Meeting, Paris, January 1983.

179 World Bank, *World Development Report*, Washington D.C., 1984.

180 *World Development*, Special Issue on Economic Stabilization in Latin America: Political Dimension, 8:11, November 1980.

181 Youssef, N. and Hetler, C., "Rural Households Headed by Women: A
Priority Concern for Development," WEP Research Working Papers,
Geneva, ILO, March 1984.

Index

Africa, 34, 45, 51, 53, 55–6, 71, 85, 86;
  eastern, 29–30;
  southern, 29–30;
  West, 35
agrarian reform, 33
agriculture, 29, 31, 32, 34, 36, 52, 61, 83,
  84, 85, 86
aid, 16–17, 39, 53, 55, 71, 73, 85
Angola, 55–6, 71
Arab Women's Studies Association
  (Beirut), 13
Argentina, 73
arms trade, 67–70
Asia, 34, 45, 54, 58;
  East, 33;
  South-East, 30
Asian and Pacific Development Center
  (APDC), 12
Asian Women's Research and Action
  Network (AWRAN), 12
Association of African Women for
  Research and Development
  (AAWORD), 12
Australia, 52

Bangalore, 9, 11
Bangkok report, 19
basic needs, 16, 17, 24, 31, 38–41, 44, 49,
  50, 57, 58, 61, 63, 66, 74, 81, 84, 85,
  86
bauxite, 30
Berg Report, 85
birth control, 48
Boserup, Ester, 30
Botswana, 56
Brazil, 12, 33, 54
Brazilian Women's Rights Council
  (São Paulo), 13
Britain, 74, 75
Bretton Woods, 59
Bucharest population conference, 47

Canada, 52
Caribbean, 30
Carlos Chagas Foundation (São Paulo),
  13
cash crops, 35, 58, 86
cassava, 57
caste, 31
Catholic church, 77
cattle ranching, 32
Central America, 32, 72
Centro de la Mujer Peruana Flora Tristán
  (Lima), 13
childcare, 23, 31, 75, 76, 80, 85, 91
children, 38, 44, 47, 57
Chile, 33, 61–2, 72, 73
China, 53
Christian Michelsen Institute (CMI), 12,
  13
CILSS (Comité Permanent Inter-états de
  lutte contre la Sécheresse dans le
  Sahel). See Club du Sahel
class, 18, 19, 21, 31, 49, 80, 87, 92
climate, 55
clinics, 41, 43
Club du Sahel and the Permanent
  Interstate Committee for Drought
  Control in the Region (CILSS), 55
cocoa, 52
coffee, 30, 32, 52
Colegio de Mexico, 13
colonialism, 25–6, 29–31, 36, 71, 73
commercialization, 25, 29, 31, 34, 35, 38,
  39, 60, 84
common lands, 35, 46, 56
computers, 36
consumer goods, 59, 61
contraception, 47–8, 77
co-operative farming, 59
copper, 30
corn, 52
cotton, 36, 37, 44, 91
crop selection, 43

Also available from Earthscan Publications Ltd:

WOMEN AND ENVIRONMENT IN THE THIRD WORLD: ALLIANCE FOR THE FUTURE

by IRENE DANKELMAN *and*
JOAN DAVIDSON

Third World women play the major role in managing natural resources. They are the hardest hit by environmental mismanagement, yet they are neither consulted nor taken into account by development strategists. This book, containing well documented case studies and interviews with leading women conservationists from the Third World, gives a clear account of women's problems in relation to land, water, forests, energy and human settlements. It also looks at the lack of response from international organizations and at the ways in which women can organize to meet environmental, social and economic challenges.

Published in association with the International Union for the Conservation of Nature and Natural Resources (IUCN).

ISBN: 1 85383 003 8

Also available from Earthscan Publications Ltd:

WORLD HUNGER: TWELVE MYTHS

by FRANCES MOORE LAPPÉ *and* JOSEPH COLLINS

"Lappé and Collins shatter deeply held myths about hunger and challenge us all to action. . . . Must reading for anyone concerned with the future of humanity" — John C. Hammock, Executive Director, Oxfam America.

"Marvelously lucid . . . swiftly demolishes the myths and powerfully arms us for the political task of ending hunger" — Dr Barry Commoner.

Every year, chronic hunger kills 18–20 million people. But why is there hunger in a world of plenty? In this revealing and often startling book, two leading experts on problems of food and agriculture demonstrate that the cause is not natural disaster, overpopulation or lack of fertile land. Examining head-on the policies that keep starving people from feeding themselves, the authors give illuminating examples of the political and social attitudes that can and must help to eliminate hunger.

ISBN: 1 85383 012 7

Also available from Earthscan Publications Ltd:

AFRICA IN CRISIS

by LLOYD TIMBERLAKE

"By far the best of the flood of volumes on the subject"
—*International Herald Tribune.*

"An incisive look at the root causes of hunger and starvation in Africa"—*Sunday Nation, Kenya.*

"A wealth of evidence backs up arguments put forward with clarity and style"—*Times of Zambia*

This influential report on the problems of drought and famine across the African continent was launched in 1985 to worldwide critical acclaim, winning the US World Hunger Media Award. Now revised and with a new introduction, Lloyd Timberlake's bestselling study is invaluable reading for anyone interested in Africa.

ISBN: 1 85383 013 5